The Art of Real Estate
IN THE DIGITAL AGE

Beyond Staging, Pricing and Open Houses

MASTERING THE 3 L'S: LOOK, LISTEN & LEARN

KEYS TO SUCCESSFUL SHORT SALES

AMAZING ANECDOTES OF REAL ESTATE

NORKA PARODI

Cover Photo Credit: Howard Austin Feld, MLS Real Estate Photography
Cover and Interior Design by JETLAUNCH.net

ISBN-10: 0-9977750-0-9
ISBN-13: 978-0-9977750-0-6

Library of Congress Control Number: 2016911166
Copia Publishing

This book is dedicated to my Abuelo Chuco whom I adored. Before he passed away over forty years ago he often said to me, "Pedacito de Carne, you must never forget that you can do anything you set your mind to." Thank you, Abuelo, for your words of wisdom that have always accompanied me.

<u>**Translation of non-English words used in my dedication:**</u>
Abuelo is grandfather in Spanish;
Chuco is a nickname for the name Jesús;
"Pedacito de Carne" is a term of endearment, just like "honey" is in the United States.

Foreword

Considering that some of the most stressful life experiences are births and deaths, in addition to buying and selling a home, *The Art of Real Estate in the Digital Age* demystifies the process of real estate in ways you may not have thought of but maybe should have. It gives the insight on a successful sale that is a win for everyone involved. Norka is committed to finding the right opportunities for her high-end clients, both buyers and sellers, and she brings this focus to her book.

I grew up in a family of real estate agents in London. My grandfather and father were highly successful in buying and selling commercial and residential real estate. However, my dad didn't succeed when he tried his hand at making deals in New York. I remember him saying that the US was for the big boys. He wasn't prepared to take the risks that had a bigger payoff. Too bad he didn't have Norka as a guide.

I met Norka in 2006, at a business conference in San Diego, CA. She carried herself with elegance, confidence, and grace. Yet speaking with her was so easy, it was like we had been friends for years. My gut instinct told me that she would be a big player in the real estate industry.

Norka is courageous and optimistic—both qualities I admire—I have been awed by her real estate knowledge and expertise. *The Art of Real Estate in the Digital Age* identifies that real estate is not stagnant but evolving. Yesterday's tools are history but important to grasp so as to guide us into tomorrow. *The Art of Real Estate in the Digital Age* will guide you to change your approach to get the opportunities you want. After you've read *The Art of Real Estate in the Digital Age*, you will feel confident and

well-equipped for your purchase or sale, whether it is a property
worth thousands or millions of dollars.

Joanna Garzilli
Scottsdale, AZ

Preface

Merriam-Webster dictionary defines art as something that is created with imagination, skill, and that is beautiful or that expresses important ideas or feelings. This is exactly what motivates me with real estate. A real estate property is a canvas where the owners or designers can create a visual lifestyle that buyers can relate to.

And even though most people don't see it, selling real estate can be an art. From negotiations to staging to open houses, a realtor creates an expression of ideas and feelings, moving the buyer to buy the property just as any art gallery would sell a masterpiece.

This is why I wrote *The Art of Real Estate in the Digital Age*. I want to show through words and my experience the emotions, ideas, and beauty that one can find in a real estate sale. And that is not to say that all real estate sales are nice. The idea of writing this book came to me a few years ago during an uncomfortable event while I was a guest at a dinner party.

I remember wearing a dazzling, crimson jacket and the sun was setting. From where I sat, I enjoyed a ZD Chardonnay while savoring the beautiful sunset. It was one of those perfect moments. I was having a great time as I watched the sunset over the Palm Beach skyline with the sun reflecting over the Intracoastal. The multitude of colors along the clear South Florida water bathed me with a peaceful rhythm; I felt a serene and calming wave flow through me. It was as if all the world's answers were at my fingertips. At that moment, I felt a peace and joy that, to this day, I continue to seek.

As they say, "All good things must come to an end." Right when I reached that perfect moment of peace, someone interrupted my tranquility with the subjects of movies and sports. From a place of harmony to the subjects of penetrating the other side's defensive line, air and ground campaigns, and something about an old movie called *Sudden Death*, my mood started to sour. Now I enjoy college football and watching movies, but the timing couldn't have been worse. Suddenly, one of the guests—a man wearing a sharp, navy suit with a gorgeous, silk, red pocket handkerchief—came out of nowhere and began to laugh with a mocking tone about a client of mine who had gone through a short sale. For the record, I never mentioned my clients' names or shared that they were going through a short sale to this guest or to anyone. I always respect my clients' privacy, so I could only guess this man knew my clients. It was at this time that another guest at the table launched into a critical tirade about people who short sell their homes. His wife gave him a nudge under the table and urged him to change the conversation. Unfortunately, she was unable to prevent him from continuing. The conversation devolved into accusing people who short sell as benefiting from entitlements, that they should know better, and they shouldn't be allowed such an "easy way out."

I was dumbstruck by their insensitive comments but sat tight-lipped. They had no knowledge or understanding of the circumstances that drove the sellers to short sell their home. Sadly, many occurrences can cause a reversal of fortune. And more often than not, they are unforeseen and unavoidable.

What these people at the table did not know was that I had personal knowledge from the seller's as well as the buyer's perspective. Good or bad, I have seen the world from both sides—and once you have experienced that, how can you possibly see things the same way again, let alone be judgmental of others?

I believe that part of life is sharing with others the knowledge that experience brings. Furthermore, part of me feels a purpose to convey different perspectives of real estate and the true meaning of home. Those are the initial reasons I wrote *The Art of Real Estate in the Digital Age*. This book is more than just about selling or purchasing a home. *The Art of Real Estate in the Digital Age* is the journey and culmination of all that I've had to overcome, a balm for my soul in written form. It is my hope that *The Art of*

Real Estate in the Digital Age will inspire you to find yourself and your home, whether that is in essence or physical form, with a positive perspective.

Contents

Introduction

Dear Reader,

For the first part of my career, I honed my entrepreneurial spirit while working for multi-billion dollar corporations outside of the United States. It was during that time that I was exposed to the world of real estate because I needed to buy a house every time I relocated.

It wasn't until the Great Recession when my division was downsized "to cut costs" that I was forced to make a choice. I was suddenly in the deep end of the real estate pool, forced to sink or swim. Slowly, my doggy paddling developed into strokes and I have been selling real estate since 2009. I closed more than 100 short sales successfully, transitioned into the luxury market, was awarded the 2015 Best Marketing Campaign for a Property by Leaders in Luxury, and also managed to survive and flourish in the foreclosure crisis of 2007 and the recession of 2008.

While the real estate market has recovered over the past few years, it remains a challenging business for both buyers and sellers for several reasons:

- The disconnect between market reality (home values) of buyers and sellers
- Constant low property appraisals that still make it difficult to complete residential real estate transactions
- Individuals still recovering financially from the Great Recession and not qualifying for loans

In this book, I offer insights gleaned from my years in the business world but also from my experiences. I suffered personal losses during the housing crisis, and that has shaped how I interact with others. In this book I share the following:

- Everything you need to know and do whether you are planning to purchase or sell a home, especially the marketing efforts and the technology now available

- How to recognize the difference between a remarkable agent and the ones who are not qualified to provide quality and responsible service

- Misconceptions about short sales, including a $120 million short sale, still considered one of the most expensive home sales in US history

- The human side of real estate through stories, both horrifying and funny, because in the end, this is a business about people, and we need to remember that regardless of circumstances, we must strive to better one another through our actions, faith, and humanity

Looking back, it feels like I have been preparing for real estate and owning my own business all my life. From the start, I knew I would succeed; therefore, I had no choice but to take the path less traveled. My real estate voyage has been an uncommon one as you will see throughout the book. I was initially overwhelmed, but I made sure that didn't impact my clients. They did not realize that I went home every night and did my homework. I began to create a name for myself by managing 20 to 40 short sales simultaneously, leaving me with literally no personal time. Then I transitioned to selling luxury real estate.

My professional involvement in the real estate industry has helped me understand all the dimensions of a home from its purest emotional and intellectual essence to its physical form. This knowledge has helped me realize that unless a buyer understands their needs and desires, they won't be able to find a home that can be their sanctuary and a place that will allow them to create the wonderful memories of life. That is why it is important to consider that all parties have a relationship in the transaction. The homeowners fall in love with the house; the realtors and the financial institution make the dream possible.

This book has three distinct phases:

- Part One is designed to show you what you need to do once you have decided to sell or buy your dream home. This section also includes information that you need to know about applying for a loan and what you should expect throughout the borrowing process.

- Part Two is specifically for individuals having trouble getting a mortgage or making mortgage payments. You will learn how to avoid the pitfalls while seeking an exit strategy. It includes details on when to elect a short sale strategy.

- Part Three is for the homeowner and focuses on what you need to know to sell your home for the highest price and how to find the most opportune buyer who will be willing to pay a premium for your unique home.

Sprinkled throughout the book are stories and anecdotes from my clients and other people who have had experience buying and selling homes. I want to arm you with necessary information, but also provide some humor so if you encounter a similar situation, you can laugh and say, "I read about this before!" and move on with a lighter heart.

I hope that you benefit from reading this book as much as I did writing it. Writing this book was an emotional rollercoaster as I looked back at many of the events I share. If you take away just one nugget of wisdom from the experiences I share in this book, then I have done my part.

Welcome to *The Art of Real Estate in the Digital Age*!

Enjoy the journey,
Norka Parodi

*"Believe In Everything Because
Everything's Reachable."*

—Justin Bieber

1

The Real Estate World as a Stage

Shakespeare famously stated "All the world's a stage and all the men and women merely players." While all men and women may be players on the stage of life, rarely do you have a clearly defined character. We all watch plays and movies with villains and heroes, but reality is often more complicated than that. There are no "villains" or "heroes" in the sale of any home, there are parties with their own interests. Ideally on a good day, everyone from seller to buyer will work to get the sale moving quickly. However, there are times when everyone will do all they can to make sure nothing happens.

On the stage of the real estate world, there are six main characters: the seller, the buyer, the real estate agent, the lender or financial institution, the closing agent, and the home. The latter being the key player. And yes, the home is a character on its own, constantly changing as time passes. I will go into more detail later on.

The Seller

I would love to write about every seller, but keeping confidentiality is one of the most valuable assets of my business. I always find the seller to be the most crucial character in every real estate transaction because a seller can make the process smooth or challenging. A seller is often the gatekeeper as they own the property. They are the ones who maintain the property and can present you with an architectural masterpiece or a design experiment. The seller is the one who might sell for a reasonable price or try to play their property as a commodity on the stock market. Finally, the seller is the one who signs the listing agreements and can facilitate or hinder a successful transaction.

Each new client brings a host of lessons. To be honest, I sometimes prefer the unconventional seller as they can be an excellent source of insight into worlds I never knew. A great example is the automobile aficionado. What do I do if I have a client who can talk about cars for hours when all I know about cars is which model the latest celebrity is driving? I learn, that's what I do. In fact, I found my dream car through one such aficionado, and I now work toward the goal of owning that car. And what if the client is obsessed with security to the extent that they only see dangers around every corner? Well, I take that as an opportunity to learn what the best security system is, safety measures that people take, and I learn just enough to ensure that I understand how to make a home secure. Turn what others see as eccentric into a source of knowledge or a path to the goal. It's all about finding a way to succeed. But what about habits considered unacceptable to some potential buyers? What you consider a harmless hobby might be offensive to a buyer, and vice versa. When selling a house, you can't let your personal lifestyle affect other spheres of your life. I am not saying that you hide your interests, but it's important to exercise common sense. Just like you dress to impress a person whose attention you intend to catch, stage your house for the buyer you expect to attract.

On more than one occasion, I have had clients who collected figurines or memorabilia. The range of collections is as diverse as something like Terminator action figures to Minnie Mouse figurines or sad clowns. All these toys in the house would end up being less attractive to a buyer who could not see past the owner's hobby. I once had a client who asked jokingly, or so I thought, "You think if I charge a small price of admission to look at my collection, I could make some money before I have to sell this house?" My client might have been joking, but the house took on qualities of a museum due to their hobby, and now I had to sell potential buyers on the idea of seeing beyond the collection. Some buyers can see past such things while others have a difficult time. What happens if you have a house full of gun memorabilia and the buyer is a gun control advocate? And before you answer, "then sell it to someone else," what if that buyer is willing to pay cash while everyone else is looking for financing? Believe it or not, these things happen, and a whole day can turn sour from one instance. If you are a homeowner contemplating the sale of your home, it is crucial to put things into perspective before putting your house on the market. Buying a home to live in is a personal decision, so cater to the buyer you are trying to seek, not to your personal whims. I will go into more detail about this in chapter 10.

A funny story that happened early on in my career in luxury real estate illustrates this. I was walking with a couple through a house that was their dream. From the moment the buyers walked in, they were swooning over all the details of the house. They loved the custom wrought iron staircase, the kitchen, etc. The husband even asked if we could negotiate for some of the furniture. I almost cried with happiness since it seemed that after only showing them two homes I was able to please my clients. Then Murphy's Law kicked in. Near the end of the tour of the house, we walked into the display room where the seller kept a collection of perfumes. And what a collection it was! In display cases covering at least half of the room were perfumes the seller had collected over a fifty-year period. For me it was fascinating to see bottles of perfumes that I had not seen in years. I thought, "What a great collection!" But what about these buyers?

For some reason, seeing the perfume collection struck a nerve. I noticed the husband's demeanor change the moment he beheld the majestic display. Everything that the husband had previously liked turned negative, and "too girly" became the words of the day. While the wife is usually the one to ultimately decide about a house, the husband threw up roadblock after roadblock every time that house was brought up. The listing agent shared with me that the owner refused to remove the display cases because they were her pride and joy. Two weeks and fourteen houses later, I showed the buyers a house that was similar in price, design, and amenities, minus the "perfume museum," and they bought it, with cash. I never asked why a collection that would not stay in the house evoked such a response. I could not believe that a hobby display stood in the way of a seller receiving almost full price. However, the incident served as a lesson. After that, I always remind my clients that the buyer buys the house they see themselves in, not the house the seller wants them to see. The house with the room displaying perfumes sold twelve months later. Sadly, the perfume collection forced the seller into paying the mortgage, taxes, and utilities for all that time. I wonder if others found the display room as disconcerting as my clients.

What if an artist owns the house and uses their home as their personal canvas? While it may sound cool to have a house that is as expressive as most of Frida Kahlo's paintings, the house must be sold, and unlike Frida Kahlo's paintings, a house with "permanent art" on the walls may not be coveted. Then again, such a property may appeal to buyers who appreciate the uniqueness, are not interested in "cookie cutter" homes, or can see past the present and look at the future possibilities.

These are some of the incidents that create the narrative of any home. From a classy New York socialite family to a Southern ranching family that loves barbecues, the house takes on the character of the homeowner as they make it their own. When you decide to sell your house you have several choices with regards to how you sell it. The first option is to transform the character of the home through staging to meet the buyers you're expecting to attract and emotionally detach from that point on. Another option, which may narrow the opportunities for you, is to sell your home without staging it and hope someone believes in its worth just like you. Finally, you can wait for "the one" to come along and buy your home, no matter how long it takes to sell. I have been lucky that most of my clients who have sold their homes stage them as I advise and are overwhelmingly happy with the results.

Did I mention that sellers are the cooperative or uncooperative type? The motives for a seller to cooperate or be an obstacle range from a cultural idiosyncrasy to a personal dislike of the agent.

When it comes to cultural differences, it is often due to a person's uncertainty if you can operate in a way they understand. Remember that we live in a world where someone from Beijing is as far away as the button of a keyboard, and this new level of globalization has advantages and disadvantages. I have had to broaden my understanding of cultures to include behaviors that I generally wouldn't accept for myself. One great example is the Latin concept of time. In South Florida we routinely joke about operating on Latino time. It may seem odd to someone from Iowa that it is socially acceptable to arrive fifteen to thirty minutes late to an appointment and, depending on the culture that tardiness may extend to business dealings. I work under the North American expectation to be on time, but some of my clients from Latin America are "fashionably late". Therefore, I make sure to set expectations while not offending the other side with my client's behavior.

The Buyer

What can I say about buyers? A seasoned, reasonable buyer with great credit who owns multiple homes all around the world and is willing to pay cash at full price is always welcome, but how many people like that do you know? From seasoned buyers to a young couple buying their first home, handling each buyer uniquely, yet with the same level of care, is a must. Without attention and empathy, what might seem okay to one buyer might cause another buyer to walk out on a deal, even if the issue is a simple misunderstanding.

I always find working with first-time buyers rewarding. When I hear that the buyers are first time homeowners, I make sure that any question they have is answered. To the first time homebuyer purchasing a home is a freedom achieved and a sense of accomplishment. Your first home is like your first kiss because you never forget it.

Many years have passed, but I still have fond memories of my first home with my ex-husband. We bought that house when I was nineteen years old. My son was born two years after and slept his first night outside the hospital in that home. My ex-husband would talk to our child and tell him how he would grow into a great man. I still remember my father-in-law giving anyone who would play any music other than classical in my son's presence a hard time because, in his words, "My grandchild will be a brilliant man and go to Harvard!" My son didn't go to Harvard, but he graduated from law school, and his grandfather is as proud as he can be. When my son has his child, I'll be the one shouting, "My grandchild will be brilliant!" It all started in that home thirty-six years ago; that's how important a first home can be.

I had the chance to see that house recently and I was shocked at how different it looked to me thirty-six years later. While the new owners repainted and basically changed the whole house, I could still picture that little home studio with our brand new, green Monte Carlo in the driveway, and it looked perfect. That was our first home and those are the memories I hope every buyer has the chance to make. The look in first-time buyers' eyes tells you they are about to embark on a new and wondrous future with a sense of the world at their feet and a can-do spirit.

There are times when buyers are unsure of what they must have, and as the agent you have to help them navigate through the unknown to narrow down the options and identify their next home. Some time ago a couple that wanted to buy their first home together contacted me. At first it was obvious they wanted different things. But in the end after understanding what was important to both, to my surprise, they bought a house that was far from their original description.

In the eyes of the Chinese, the number 4 is generally disliked by people just as number 13 is in the western world. This is because the number 4 in Chinese is homophonous to the word 死 which means "death." For that reason many high-rise buildings in East Asia don't include the fourth, fourteenth and twenty-fourth floors and other floors with the number 4.

I have also had amazing opportunities to work with seasoned buyers who know what they want and because you know the area, you become their advisor. I recently had a married couple as clients. The husband asked if I knew a spa where he could take his wife. I recommended one. The next day after showing them the last home they surprised me with a gift for services to my favorite spa in Boca Raton.

Another thing to consider with buyers is their culture. While we live in a global community, you only need to travel from Miami, FL to Boston, MA to see how different the cultures of two regions in the *same* country are. Even though they have the same currency, same language (most of the time), and same laws, people in each city can be like night and day. You need only look at the foods eaten, the fashion styles, and the dialects of each region to see two very different parts of the same country. Now imagine this difference put on a global scale where not only the language is different, but so are the ways of thinking and doing business. Understanding these fundamental differences is crucial when working with international buyers and this helps prevent you from committing cultural No-Nos. One example of a cultural No-No would be showing properties with the number four in the address to a buyer from China. Christopher Kai, a networking expert and author of *Big Game Hunting: Networking with Billionaires, Executives and Celebrities*, once explained to me that the word for

Figure 1 shows an elevator in China illustrating Chinese superstition with the omission of floors with the number 4.

Photo taken by David Davies from Museum Fatigue

the number 4 in Chinese sounds similar to the word for "death". This helped me later in a business deal where a Chinese business-man appreciated my cultural "understanding" and confirmed what Christopher had told me. In addition, it confirmed the obvious; his previous agent had made that very mistake. If I was Chinese and a realtor showed me a house that had the word "death" in it, I would fire that realtor right away, wouldn't you?

I take pride in taking the time to understand other cul-tures, but there are times when my beliefs or lack of knowledge have made me realize I am always learning. A great example is the swastika. In some Asian cultures it is meant to be a symbol of peace, but being Jewish, I would never live in a house with a swastika. When my son went off to law school he lived next to a neighbor who drew a swastika in front of their townhouse. When I went to visit him I was disgusted by what I saw until my son's friend who is Korean explained that my son's neighbor was Korean as well, and in that culture the swastika means some-thing completely different. Since I have had the opportunity to be exposed to people from all over the world I have learned the importance of recognizing that respecting cultural differences leads to proper communication. You will see throughout this book the importance of ample communication and clear expectations.

The Real Estate Agent

In *Following the Equator*, Mark Twain mentioned, "There are three kinds of people—Commonplace Men, Remarkable Men, and Lunatics." Even though I would exchange the word "Luna-tics" with "Reckless Men," real estate agents can be similarly cat-egorized. You want the Remarkable Agent because those agents serve their customers. They spend time keeping up to date with new market trends and they know how to effectively market online and offline to the most opportune buyers. In addition, they know how to appropriately price your home to sell within a rea-sonable time frame. Even though the remarkable agent takes cal-culated risks based on empirical data, they also act as an advisor and not as someone who tells you only what you want to hear. I recently dealt with an agent who made sure to serve his client. We both decided that in the best interest of our respective clients, their lawyers should be involved while negotiating the price because of the disparity of our clients' positions. We even interviewed the appraisers together. Our conversations were heated at times, but we worked together for each client's interest. In the end we successfully closed the deal because we had our egos in check. Success during negotiations is when having a remarkable agent pays off.

The Commonplace Agent can't provide advice because they don't spend the time looking for the answers. Instead they rely on dishonesty, gimmicks or power plays. This type of agent can't negotiate deals because they likely have not have taken the time to gain a clear understanding of their clients' goals. Their approach is to make the other party look unreasonable. I must say that even more troublesome is that they do not take the time to prioritize since not all goals, needs, and wants carry the same weight. In the end the Commonplace Agent gives the real estate industry a bad name. To give an example, in one of my short sale transactions, the buyer's agent never disclosed the marital relationship the agent had with the buyer. The agent was willing to sign an arm's length affidavit that could have caused us legal trouble if the relationship had not been discovered prior to closing. And his response when confronted with the dilemma was, "No one told me, this is how I always do it."

One of the meanings of "Lunatic" is "a person whose actions and manners are marked by extreme eccentricity or recklessness." I believe the use of the word reckless applies because that type of agent tries to bend the law or completely break it at your expense and mine, if allowed.

I have a rule which I apply to each real estate transaction: it is imperative to make sure the license of the agent is active and in good standing prior to fully executing the contract. It is also necessary to check the status of the agent's license a second time in preparation for closing. Thanks to that rule, when I was selling the property of one of my clients I found out that even though the agent had an active license at the beginning of the sale transaction, at the time the contract was executed the agent's license was not active. Once I found out I communicated this to the agent and the broker. To make a long story short, the buyer had to hunt for an agent with an active license in Florida before closing. Why is this step important in my industry? Conducting real estate business without an active license is a third-degree felony in Florida.

If that is not enough to raise your eyebrows, I have a story of another encounter with a reckless agent. I was the seller's agent. An agent with an involuntarily, inactive license sent an offer to my office. Upon receipt, I called the agent with the inactive license and explained that a person without an active license could not receive any compensation, nor could I do business with him without committing a felony. I could not believe the nerve of that person to argue while defending his actions. Afterward, he abruptly hung up the phone. Despite the TV show, to me prison orange is *not* the new black.

The Lender or Financial Institution

Whether you are getting a loan, paying off the mortgage, or are in the middle of a short sale, from my perspective the financial process of buying a home can be as simple as providing the information requested by the lender or as complicated as having to explain every aspect and anomaly of your life in detail. It does not matter if you are a buyer seeking a loan or a homeowner seeking a short sale of your home. present the information as completely as possible and in a format that makes it easy for the processor. Keep a copy of everything you provide since there is always the possibility of human error. Another recommendation is to restrain yourself even when you feel like pulling your hair out. Like my mother used to say, "You can catch more flies with sugar and honey than with vinegar." Not that the lender's representative is a fly, but you know what I mean.

The financial institution/lender character has several components: mortgage lenders, brokers, and servicers. Your mortgage lender is the financial institution that loans you the money. A mortgage loan broker acts as an intermediary between the borrower and lender for the purpose of a loan origination.

Once the loan is issued, a mortgage servicer handles the day-to-day tasks of managing your loan. Your loan servicer typically processes your loan payments, responds to borrower inquiries, keeps track of principal and interest paid, manages your escrow account, and may initiate foreclosure if you miss too many loan payments. Your servicer may or may not be the same company that gave you the loan. This can be confusing when dealing with a short sale or when disputes with your financial institution occur, but I will go into more detail in a later chapter.

The Closing Agent

This character, on the world stage, can be the difference between the sale of a home or a botched closing. A seasoned closing agent can make everything go smoothly and efficiently. I would argue that they are second in importance only to the sellers themselves, as they provide information to any lenders or financial institutions for closing, order the title searches to understand what is required to clear the title and transfer a marketable title, and make sure to disburse funds to each designated party on the settlement statement. I don't want you to think that is all they do since there is a lot more the closing agent does behind the scenes. The best way to put it is if the listing agent is the quarterback in a football game, the closing agent is the wide receiver or running back who runs the ball into the end zone.

The Home

A house comes in many forms, from great ones to those in need of upgrades or repairs. Still, in any sale the house is the center of attention for all parties involved. The house is more than just four concrete walls and a roof in a residential transaction. To all the parties in an investment sale, it is simply a matter of numbers with no emotions involved, but to the family that is planning to live in it the house is an extension of them.

To the seller, the house is a realm of memories such as the place where the children grew up or where the owners lovingly cared for their parents as they moved into their twilight years. The house is a place of refuge that gave the owner a sense of purpose. Even the most slovenly homeowner cherishes their home because of the freedom and the dream it represents.

The seller sets the tone for the house. The character of a house is set by how it looks, feels, and is presented. This is important to the buyer. The buyer can look at the house from various angles. They can range from a first time buyer to a couple starting anew after going through their own short sale several years before. The buyer will add their unique story and set a new tone that adds to a home's overall character.

Conclusion

When all of the characters in the world of selling and buying a property work together, they make the sale transaction a good experience, and when they don't, the experience may leave a sour taste for one or all parties involved.

Throughout this book I will share with you some of my experiences and examples from my history about how things can go right or wrong. When you read about what can go wrong in a sale, remember the adage "those who don't learn from history are fated to repeat it." I tell you this because I wish for you to learn from my mistakes and those of the people in my book. But above all I wish that everything transpires smoothly when you decide to buy or sell a home. And even if it doesn't go well, I want you to realize there is always a good path forward.

"If you were born without wings, do nothing to prevent them from growing."

—Coco Chanel

2

The Adventures of a Buyer

While viewing a house just bought for the newlyweds for the first time, a young nineteen-year-old girl naively said to her husband, "Wow, this looks like a doll house." I was that young newlywed and I know now I should never have said something so insulting. I grew up in a house that my dad had built in Puerto Rico. My dad, a civil engineer by trade, built this mammoth home in a neighborhood where other young professionals and businessmen lived with their families. I realize that now, but while growing up a very large home was normal to me.

Growing up in that house was great because I have a lot of wonderful memories and most important, it allowed me to dream! Some of the memories that I cherish the most are when my brother, sisters and friends who lived in my neighborhood walked home from school and passed by Luis Muñoz Marín's residence. Marín was a politician and statesman and he is regarded as the "Father of Modern Puerto Rico." He moved the island from an occupied territory to a bustling commonwealth, thereby giving Puerto Ricans nearly all the same rights that a US state has, save for a few unique distinctions that I won't go into in this book.

How can I dismiss my desire to find out what the Marín residence looked like? My imagination allowed me to perceive it as a modern residence with large windows surrounded by beautiful gardens full of white orchids and exotic birds. I also imagined a stable full of Paso Fino horses providing him the opportunity to ride his horses as the liberator he was.

As an adult I have seen the Luis Muñoz Marín's residence and even though some of my imagination served me right, most of the home was very simple with old furniture and small windows. There were nice gardens but nothing exotic. There was no stable, just acres of unadulterated nature. In the end looking at the home was insightful and it taught me a lesson. The house exemplified the man who lived in it and his style. It was truly an extension of his persona, no different than any other home that assumes the character of the owners.

As for me, I can truly say that my childhood home was the essence of my family. It had ample space to play and included a fully equipped dollhouse and a music room where we could play guitar, piano, or the organ. Looking back I can understand how my naive words hurt a young man who was just trying to provide a home for his newlywed wife. I understand the adverse impact those words had on my ex-husband. But most importantly, this is a perfect example of the many misconceptions and expectations first-time buyers may have.

Setting Expectations

As a realtor one of the key factors to success is to make sure to set expectations from the beginning. Whether a first-time buyer or an experienced homeowner, I make sure to educate my client and go over what is at stake. Clients engage with me mainly because of my expertise and guidance. Therefore, my first rule is to go through the process and explain how to prepare to buy a house. In addition, I set the expectations and explain what might happen throughout the sale. But before we get into that there are some things that a buyer must consider. For instance, if you are a first time buyer you will benefit from distinguishing your needs and wants. So before you go house hunting, take the time to brainstorm a list of what you must have in your new home and which

features are simply nice extras to have. Some of the must-haves
may include:

- Number of bedrooms and bathrooms
- Proximity to your work and other places you frequent
- Access to main roads and your preferred school districts
- The need to live in a golf community

Keep in mind that every neighborhood is different and it
could change from one block to another. For example, in the city
of Boca Raton, Florida where I live, there are various country club
communities that require equity membership. In some of these
communities the equity membership required upfront could easily be an extra $50,000 to $90,000 and that can't be financed as
part of the mortgage. The member dues may be another $10,000
to $30,000 per year. Another type of neighborhood prevalent in
Florida is 55+ Communities. In these age-restricted communities minors are treated more often as vagrants than visitors. They
require at least one of the buyers to be 55 years of age or older
at the time of purchase. I remember assisting a couple and every
house I showed them they dismissed because there were always
kids next to the house I was showing them. They would com-
plain about "too much noise" at the mere sight of a child in the
neighborhood. I ended up showing them various 55+ Communities where children were not an issue. Another couple I worked
with had a different situation. Their grandchildren would come to
stay every summer. For them living in a 55+ Community was not
feasible.

If outdoor living is important to you, the amount of outdoor
space or having a pool in the back yard or the space to build one
might be things to consider. Another point to consider might be
if you are open to a fixer-upper or some remodeling due to the
appealing location of the home. Keep in mind that everything has
a dollar sign associated with it.

The other things that you, the buyer, may have on your wish
list are just nice to have:

- House with well-manicured landscaping
- House that is decorated to your taste
- Anything else you can easily fix or install by yourself

In end, it's key to define your must-haves and nice-to-haves because it will help you identify your needs.

Identifying Your "Exclusive Buyer's Agent"

It is important that you have an agent who works with you and looks out for your best interests. For that reason identify your "exclusive buyer's agent"; this agent will assist you through the process and may help you identify the professionals you need on your team for an easy transition throughout the home buying process. If you were planning to use the listing agent you might be asking yourself, "Why should another agent be brought into the transaction when one agent can handle the entire sale and save some money?" Simple, most sellers list their homes through an agent—but those agents work for the seller. They're paid based on a percentage so their interest will be in getting the best terms and highest price for the seller. I often notice that some potential buyers come to me hoping that I will give them a break by negotiating a lower sale price just to work with both the buyer and the seller. Here is where the selection process becomes necessary. A dedicated listing agent must always have their client's best interest as the priority.

In Florida most real estate brokerages are transactional which means they are not legally responsible to the buyer or the seller. The only thing the law requires in the state of Florida is for transaction brokerages to act with honesty and fairness in all transactions and exercise due care and skill in their work. Perhaps this is the reason some buyers feel they can get a lower price and save some money.

I remember some time ago a potential buyer who was not being represented by an agent came to one of my open houses. The property was listed for over $1 million. He kept asking me to do all this research for him and he constantly challenged me to justify the list price and I did. But he kept valuing the property differently. After several weeks of talking with him he finally decided to stop beating around the bush and he made an offer, $200,000 less than the fair market value. He justified his obscenely low offer by telling me that since he was not represented by another agent, it was in my best interest to get the seller on board so I could work with both sides. He was so smug about the offer. Imagine his face when I told him that doing that would jeopardize my integrity and that I was not willing to do that. I presented the offer to the homeowner but shared my experience. In the end, we both had a good laugh when I sold the house for $300,000 above that lowball offer. I understand that as realtors we need to make a living and a few thousand dollars extra is no laughing matter. But as business professionals if we sell our integrity just for a buck we become a commodity that can be bought and sold just like copper or coffee. I believe in applying this same level of professionalism when representing the buyer. Now that I have gotten that off my chest it is time to get off my soapbox.

Secure a Loan

The next thing that I recommend you do is to determine what you can afford. It is not uncommon to eat more than our stomach can hold, and that's why someone invented Alka-Seltzer. But buying beyond your means can lead to financial ruin as well as an upset stomach.

If you are not planning to pay cash for the home, obtaining a mortgage pre-approval from the lender is a must. Therefore, call your mortgage broker or lender and move quickly if you have not already done so. This is when you decide whether to go with a fixed rate or adjustable rate mortgage and whether to pay points. And there are other expenses that you need to keep in mind outside of the home loan. Expect to pay around $50 for a credit check at this point. Most of the other fees will be due at the closing. Expect the appraisal to be part of your closing costs. It will be approximately $375 for an appraisal of the home in the case of a conventional or VA loan. In the case of an FHA loan expect the appraisal to cost you $450. And if your loan is a Jumbo loan or Jumbo VA, expect the appraisal to cost you $600.

If you're using FHA financing (almost one-fifth of buyers get FHA-insured loans) your home payment can't exceed 31 percent of your monthly income when using a direct lender. Keep in mind that with any FHA loan or with a down payment under 20 percent, you will pay for private mortgage insurance (PMI), a safety net protecting the bank in case you fail to make payments. PMI adds about 0.8 percent of the total loan amount to your mortgage payments for the year.

For conventional loans a safe formula is that home expenses (such as taxes, insurance, utilities, and mortgage) should not exceed 36 percent of your gross monthly income. Therefore, before you start shopping make sure you know what you can afford. The worst thing that can happen is that you find your dream house and later fall into disillusion because you can't afford it.

Financing and Other Fees You Never Thought Of

As a first time buyer you may not be aware of certain fees and closing costs. These may include the appraisal fee, loan fees, attorney's fees, inspection fees, and the cost of a title search. They can quickly add up to 5-6 percent of the purchase price (not the mortgage amount). I once worked with a first time buyer who thought that buying a home was as simple as those car commercials on TV telling you to "sign and drive" and she nearly cried when she learned the real costs of buying a home. She tried to cut costs by not ordering an inspection as well as other cost saving measures. Thankfully, she eventually took my advice and spent the money on inspections, and she was glad she did when the inspection uncovered mold and other issues that were not visible to the average person. She was able to renegotiate the purchase price of her home and came out ahead, even after factoring in the cost to remediate the mold. This buyer's story is not the norm of course, but these kinds of things happen enough that it is worth taking into account and budgeting for all these safety items.

Home Shopping: The Quest Begins

This is the fun part because you look on the internet like most people do and/or you get the listings from your agent. Either way this is a lot of fun for you and a lot of effort for the agent doing the research to help you find your dream home. You also need to make a good-faith deposit—usually 1 to 10 percent of the purchase price—into an escrow account. If you talk to real estate agents it is not uncommon to hear them talk about having to show 20 to 30 homes before finding the right one for any particular buyer. But what some agents forget to share are some of the great stories that can happen from seeing those homes.

If Only I Had Taken Photos

I must share that previewing or showing houses can be a lot of fun. The only regret I have is that I never took photos of these "unique" showings. I remember one listing with four separate lockboxes and all from the same agent. Somehow the agent felt it was necessary to place them one on top of the other. And if that was not enough, there was a doorknob and door latch that had to be opened at the same time in order to open the door. It took me some time to realize that both had to be turned and pressed at the same time. This resulted in a laugh from my buyers as they spent some time trying to figure out what the seller had in mind by installing this convoluted system.

Another home looked interesting enough until we realized that every room had a different type of tile and none of them were matching or interchangeable. Even worse, the minute you walked in the kitchen you had four distinct types of tile all within a three foot distance of each other. There was white tile in the hall, pink tile in the kitchen, reddish-orange tile in the family room, and a brownish tile in the master bedroom. The master bedroom door was less than five feet from the kitchen, I might add. While this would be perfect if you were in the tile business, the fact that all these types of multi-colored tiles converged in the same spot without any discernible reason looked like a designer's worst nightmare.

The funniest showing of that day was a house where the broker remarks instructed the listing had an electronic box known in the real estate industry as Supra. While at the property, we found out the Supra was missing the key. And even funnier was to find out the listing office knew about this and directed me to use the lock box underneath, never bothering to note the change on the MLS.

But of all the inconceivable things I have seen when previewing a house, the most amazing was a living room storing car parts that were being shipped to Brazil. The mountain consisting of car parts was close to the ceiling. I probably should have taken a photo but I was so surprised by the site that I did not. Seeing the amount of car parts took me back to the time when I was walking through a partly demolished building in Anchieta, Brazil. I was visiting the structure to decide the best place to put the data center for the Ryder logistics operations for Volkswagen. I remember the intense smell of metal and grease as I passed through that building, looking up to see half the sky exposed and birds cawing from the rafters. Unlike the time in Brazil, this mound of parts was in a living room right here in Florida. No birds were cawing from the ceiling this time, but the smell of metal and grease was unmistakable. There are times I show homes and I am amazed the way people function within the confinement of a residence. Those times show that the meaning of home is different for everyone.

Home Inspection: A Must, Not a Maybe!

I always recommend my clients have the home they are intending to purchase inspected. An inspection costs anywhere from $350 to $1,000 for a more detailed one. And it may take two or more hours. In my experience, the cost of an inspection is well worth it.

I recommend you, the buyer, attend the inspection because you will learn a lot about the overall condition of the property like the construction materials used, wiring, and heating. Also, the inspector may identify major problems like a roof that needs to be replaced, the existence of toxic black mold, toxic Chinese drywall, etc. The results of the inspection are a great tool for renegotiations. You will either want the seller to fix the problem before you move in or deduct the cost of the repairs from the sale price. If the seller doesn't agree to either remedy the issue or reduce the price to compensate for the issue, you may decide to walk away from purchasing the house, which you can do without penalty if you have that contingency written into the purchase contract.

The Community and Its Association

If you are planning to purchase a home in any community governed by an association, the first thing you should do is obtain copies of the governing documents, including the Covenants, Conditions & Restrictions, and read these documents carefully. Furthermore, if you find the documents cumbersome or you do not understand them, consult an attorney for guidance.

It is essential that prospective buyers realize that homeowners agree to comply with these association regulations when they move into an association-governed community. These rules normally apply to assessments, architectural guidelines (such as additions and property paint colors), landscaping, maintenance, any future renters, pets, and much more. And some people have a hard time when faced with rules that are enforced to maintain established community regulations.

I suggest you examine the financial strength of the association carefully because it sets the level of assessments and services. Additionally, make sure you ask yourself questions about the community's impact on your personal life. Does the community fit your lifestyle? I live in one of those golf communities with no tee time required. I must admit that we love the excellent service we get at the country club, the beautiful scenery, and the sense of security a gated community offers. But my significant-other bristles when faced with some of the rules of the community; little things like having to wear a tie or jacket during an event is something he has a hard time with. If you are one of those who hate to wear a jacket and tie, make sure you understand the rules of the country club community because they may or may not be right for you.

If you view any neighborhood as an extension of the personalities and character of the people who live in it, then you realize that you must first figure out who you are in essence. Only then you will be able to make a fair assessment of the impact on your life and that of your family. The reason being, in the end, any community is an opportunity for connectedness. The reason is simple: relationships in any given community can be so close and intense that they make it easy to project on another person that which we cannot abide in ourselves, making it necessary to seriously consider the various factors that make the community the right fit for you and your family.

Final Walk-Through

The walk-through inspection prior to closing allows you to conduct an inspection of the property within 24 hours of the closing. During one of my sales the walk-through gave my client the opportunity to realize the homeowner had removed the refrigerator from the house. My client had taken photos of the appliances and I had noted the serial numbers. We requested to delay the closing until after the refrigerator was brought back into the house. The seller complied and the closing took place the following day.

"A successful sale is the product of the realtor's time, dedication, and experience expended BEFORE the house is listed."

—Norka Parodi

3

Is the Seller Serious?

One of the most significant lessons I learned while listing my first "luxury property" was to make sure some conditions were met: the seller should be committed to sell and not motivated to list just to test the market, and the seller should be realistic about the actual value of their home and ready to show the property. That was a $7,000-plus lesson I won't ever forget. And that was just the amount of money spent in marketing that property, which did not take into account any of my time devoted to the project, my assistant's salary, gasoline, etc.

"I want to schedule an appointment for us to go over the offer I just received. When will you have time to meet?" I communicated to my client.

"That's great! Tell me a little bit more about the offer. I have time now to go over the details of the offer. We do not need to meet in person. I don't view it as necessary," my client responded. At that point an awkward feeling started to take hold in the pit of my stomach, but I ignored it.

Joyously, I began, "Well, I am pleased to say that not only is the offer meeting the asking price, it is also a cash offer with great terms. It's everything you want. In fact, I also have the check for escrow that came with the offer." I told my client about the deal with confidence, certain that they would feel the same way I did, even when I rarely speak in such an absolute manner. I continued, "As I understand from the buyers' agent, the buyers are relocating soon and need to close within thirty days." Worrying about the possible issue of closing in thirty days, I asked, "Is thirty days enough for you to move all your belongings? I recall you saying that you would move for the right offer." I was so sure that I had negotiated the right offer for my client that I could never have been ready for what happened next.

After a long pause my client spoke, "Well, since you were able to get a full price offer so quickly, wouldn't it be better to hold out and see if we can get a higher offer? I would like to raise the price and get more. I truly believe we can get more. Don't you think so, too?"

Dumbfounded, I responded, "I don't believe so, the list price is already above the fair market value of other houses, and we will be setting the record as the highest home sale in the neighborhood for this type of house." From that point on, my discussion with my client went awry and my client outright refused to sell in the end. I should have followed that initial feeling in the pit of my stomach and found a way to engage them in person.

I consider myself a nurturing person and maybe that is the reason I put my heart and soul into my listings. But early in my career as a realtor, I experienced several instances where my efforts were met with my client's apathy or irrational logic. It was then that I finally learned I could not help someone sell their home if they are not committed to moving forward. I learned to use my initial engagement with any prospective client to determine their true intentions.

Years ago I had a client who kept disregarding the bank's requests for documents within forty-eight hours. I had to continuously explain the importance of cooperation with the short sale process by providing the necessary documentation in a timely manner. It did not seem to matter that every delay made it more difficult to keep the process moving forward. The day finally came when the negotiator closed the file, and there was not enough time to complete the short sale process prior to the judicial sale.

Just like in the scenarios above, the homeowners had signed a listing agreement stating they wanted to sell their home, but they were not serious about selling. I learned quickly that one of my many roles as a realtor is to make sure to work with homeowners who are genuinely motivated to sell, whether it is a traditional resale of a home or a short sale.

The Start of the Relationship With the Homeowner

As I have indicated in chapter 2, I find that a key factor to success is to make sure to set expectations from the beginning. Whether a first-time buyer, an experienced homebuyer, or a short-sale buyer, I make sure to educate my client and go over what is at stake. Clients engage with me, not just to sell their real estate property for the best and highest price, but also for my expertise and guidance. I also find that when I go over the various steps and expectations I weed out some of the clients who are not serious.

A Seller Within My Own Skin

I can truly say that I understand the different parties in the sale of a home. After all I am a realtor, and in my previous profession I relocated every two or three years looking for career growth. But looking back even though relocating that often was hard on my family, it was easier than the last two real estate transactions I experienced personally. The first uncomfortable real estate transaction was right after my divorce and the second one resulted from the need to avoid foreclosure. Both instances carried high levels of stress and mixed feelings at times. I recall that it was not until the sale took place that feelings of relief mixed with shame occupied most of my thoughts. I can honestly say the last one was by far the hardest, but once I met the family buying my home, it made it easier because I felt they would cherish the house as much as I did.

Regardless of the circumstances and reasons to sell, your life does not end when you sell your home. Leaving your home is always hard no matter the type of sale, but it can be an opportunity to open the door to new beginnings just like it was for me.

Emotions of a Home

Even in situations where both parties on the note, mortgage, and deed are married and living in the same house, don't assume that everyone is on board. The purchase or sale of a home is often tied to the emotional center of people's lives. For some, the property is more than just an investment that can fluctuate in value; it represents their ability to sustain their life and sense of self-worth.

If one spouse doesn't want to sell he or she may choose to stay in the house during showings and perform subtle sabotages by making comments, giving the buyer strange looks, or even cooking or eating food with an unappealing smell. It is hard enough to convince the buyer to walk through a property with the homeowner present, but a pungent odor can kill any possibility of a sale.

If there are tenants make sure they are ready and willing to relocate when the property sells. Sometimes tenants refuse to cooperate at all and others cooperate with restrictions. I had one tenant restrict showing times to just one hour per week, always in the evenings. Another only opened the property for showings one day per week. I decided to deal with these difficulties and in both instances; the properties were so hot that I received several offers above the asking price. Again, not all of these stories have happy endings. If you have tenants make it worthwhile for them to cooperate and leave right at closing. You will have an easier time with the transition.

Thought Provoking Questions

1. If you are planning to sell your home, are you committed? Are your intentions to test the market?

2. If you are planning to purchase a home, do you actually know what you can afford? Is being house poor okay for you?

These are some of the questions you should be able to answer prior to engaging a professional. And be honest with the agent, some will spend the time with you even if you are only testing the market.

I have a client who contacted me over two years ago. At the time he was just thinking about selling and was not sure if he would get what he invested in upgrading his home. This was at a time when short sales in South Florida were hot and in high demand. Today is a different market with scarce inventory and his house is in a great location and in great condition. He decided now is his time to sell and guess who is listing it for him. Like I said earlier, just share your intentions with agents while shopping for one.

"Selling is essentially a transfer of feelings."

—Zig Ziglar

4

Win-Win-Win Outcomes

Listing, pricing, staging, marketing, and showing the home are some of the most important elements that need to be executed cohesively to sell a property in any market. When they are not cohesive and done well, the foundation is flawed. This is where my idea of win-win-win outcomes in real estate originates.

In my business I incorporate many of the concepts I honed during my years in Corporate America. After all, real estate is a business and a contact sport. It was there that I learned about successful transactions where both the buyer and seller leave feeling the transaction was a success. In any real estate transaction there are several players: realtors, lenders/financial institutions, buyers, sellers, and closing agents. Is there a way for everyone to win? Absolutely, win-win-win outcomes occur when each party involved in the real estate transaction feels they have won. In this type of scenario, each side benefits and any resolutions to the conflict are likely to be accepted voluntarily. The process of integrative bargaining aims to achieve, through open communication and cooperation, win-win-win outcomes. These outcomes may take time, money, cooperation, and perhaps relationships, but in my opinion, integrative bargaining is the best approach.

You may be asking yourself, what does win-win-win have to do with listing, pricing, staging, marketing, and showings? Well, it is everything. This concept is not new for people in business, specifically for those in service organizations where some of the services a company provides are outsourced to a third party. If you are a realtor looking to meet with your prospective client to list a property, you have to make sure you put on your consulting hat and take the time to educate and guide your client in today's market.

This win-win-win approach helped me while dealing with other agents and lenders at the beginning of my career in the real estate industry. Let's keep in mind that I started in real estate in 2009, and at that time all you could find, for the most part, were short sales. Back then I found that successful realtors who handled distressed properties had mastered the art of pricing short sale residences to satisfy both the investor, who owned the note, and seller. Furthermore, mastering pricing for short sales in the luxury market was as important as understanding how to present a seller's lender a winning business proposition so the investor would accept a loss. Knowing how to do both successfully was essential to closing the short sale transaction. That was the foundation of my win-win-win mentality.

The win-win-win for all parties involved is simple in concept, yet it takes effort to do it right. You need to create a value for the home as well as for everyone involved. This simple concept may seem obvious when you discuss proper pricing and staging, but when you break down all that goes into creating that value, it is anything but obvious. It is the same principle I used when working for fortune 500 companies, there was a win-win but in real estate there is more involved than just business to business relationships. The bottom line is that the win-win-win mentality for all parties involved works in any industry.

It's About Creating Value

Regardless of who you are, you most likely agree with me that selling real estate successfully is all about finding a perfect match between a property and a buyer. I believe that regardless of the price point, everyone expects value, and even more so for high-net-worth individuals because they are used to hiring professionals to advise them. And yes, that is part of their DNA whether they purchase a small rental property to add to their portfolio or a luxury home. Furthermore, most of the billionaires in the US are self-made; therefore, they tend to approach real estate as a business transaction. Realtors who have mastered the luxury market create value and the principle can be applied to all price points of the real estate market. I always viewed the creation of value as the core to generate customer trust; it is no different than what consultants do. Therefore, my strategy is to always provide value to all parties in the transaction. Even when I dealt with short sales I knew buyers had to perceive a value when they were purchasing, the third-party

> I love Sir Henry Royce famous quote "The Quality will remain long after the price is forgotten." I am a firm believer that quality-minded service sets remarkable agents apart from the rest.

servicer had to mitigate the loss for their investor, and the sellers obviously wanted to get the deficiency forgiven and move forward with their lives. Regardless of the price of the home and the type of property, to get the most money for your property, it's important to hire a realtor who knows how to market the property to identify the right buyer. This type of marketing specialist has the credentials as well as the experience to put together a well-thought, choreographed plan that encompasses the listing, pricing, staging, and marketing strategies. Otherwise, your property will sit on the market for a long time, jeopardizing the ability to procure viable offers to ensure a successful closing that satisfies you.

Identify the Right Buyer

A successful agent will know not only how to identify and procure the most appropriate buyer, but also how to create an atmosphere where that buyer is willing to pay top dollar for that home which is a "must have." The reason being that to the right buyer the fear of loss is a major factor; I see it all the time. I just had a listing that sold for over $200,000 more than any property sold in that neighborhood since that community's inception. How did

I achieve that? It was not by luck, I can assure you. The first step was to create a list of all the amenities and unique features the home had to offer. That list was used to identify the most suitable candidates to attract. One of the selling factors the home had was the smart home features, and in today's market there are affluent/savvy buyers looking for that. The buyer who understood the unique value of this home purchased it, and believe me, there is always one out there. In the end it is all about needs and wants. Therefore, identifying the most opportune buyer is crucial, next to the right level of negotiations.

The Price Is Right; Or Is It?

In residential real estate, regardless of the tier of the market you are in, the asking price is always something that is critical. It is also one of the most challenging parts of the industry. And it's not as simple as sticking your fingers in the air to see which way the wind blows to formulate a price. I find that price is psychological more than anything else. In this section I will discuss some of the best practices.

Sellers often overestimate the worth of their home because of the emotional factor of it. Successful agents master the art of pricing residences while working with eager sellers to concur on a price. Proper pricing creates a momentum when a new listing comes to the market. That first month is key in a traditional resale because the longer the home sits on the market, the price starts to drop in the buyer's eyes. Keep in mind this is not true in properties worth millions of dollars. The sale time is much longer in those.

In the traditional market the usual practice is for the listing agent to pull prior sales of comparable properties when selling a property. Some agents take it a step further and analyze the trends of properties sold during periods of time. In addition, they identify any anomalies to estimate a range of the fair market value. Doing so allows identifying the type of market. Since markets are cyclical you can recognize which phase the market is in by noting the values properties are selling for. You will be able to tell if the market is increasing or decreasing. Identify the amenities and it will give you an idea of the best suitable type of buyer.

Another factor that affects price is scarcity; when the inventory in a desirable neighborhood is low, comparable prices become less relevant. I know of an elderly community where a clever property owner keeps purchasing properties, fixing them, and bringing the value of the community to a new level. In this community there is an unusually low inventory coupled with a clever owner and his agent who understand how to work that neighborhood. Even though this is on the low side of the spectrum for some people, a net gain of $40,000 is still a gain for the seller and a quick commission for the agent.

As I indicated earlier, residential real estate is more about psychology. Buyers like to feel that they are getting a good deal regardless of the market because that is the way the human brain works. An excellent example of this is a buyer I worked with some time ago on a luxury sale. This buyer was a true bargain hunter, even when the situation wouldn't allow it. I once presented him with a luxury property that I thought was well priced and would fit him perfectly. He agreed that the home fit him and his family to the letter, except for the price. He would not back down from offering $50,000 less than what the seller's bottom line was. This buyer remained obstinate, going so far as to say, "I'll hold off for six months. He won't get that house sold and he'll be begging me to make my offer." The buyer didn't have to wait six months because the property was sold within a month for the price I had advised him. Why? There was a scarcity in the neighborhood coupled with amenities buyer were willing to pay for.

Advice to New Agents Regarding Overpriced Listings

There is a cute saying in real estate that it is better to be someone's first love, their second wife, or their third realtor. The first time I heard the saying, I thought it was odd, but boy it is so true. Sometimes it is better to let someone else get the overpriced listing because it is not until the sellers have gone through over-pricing disappointments with one or two agents that they are ready to listen and to work with their realtor.

There are situations where taking listings that are pushing the envelope regarding pricing are necessary. During times when I have broken pricing records, some of my colleagues, as well as some buyers, thought the property was overpriced for whatever reason. But once I was able to prove the unique value or premium amenities those properties had to offer, I made sure to highlight the uniqueness to the most opportune buyers in the right market. Therefore, to be successful in this industry you have to become adept at knowing when to take an overpriced listing and when to pass.

You have to evaluate if you have the right market conditions to set record breaking prices. For example, there may be an over-priced listing in an area where all the properties are the same. In other words, in a tract housing development the builder is still building brand-new homes, but the potential seller wants to sell a property $100,000 over the fair market value just because. This is not a good idea. You will spend unnecessary marketing money and effort and you won't be able to create momentum because of the surplus of properties.

In the end your goal as the listing agent is to create the best conditions to deliver the highest price possible; and that will greatly depend on your marketing strategy, unique amenities, demand, as well as the cycle. During the times I focused on listing short sales, I always strived to get the best and highest sale price in spite of the recession.

Pricing the Luxury and Ultra-Luxury

Pricing high-end properties is more of an art because numbers become theoretical and often elastic. Every luxury property and ultra-luxury estate are as unique as a Picasso portrait or Richard Neutra home. These properties are difficult to assess, therefore, pricing them properly requires experience and the use of sound judgment in weighing all market data and nuances. There are a lot of intangibles to consider. Some are uniqueness, architectural significance, exclusive amenities, quality of finishes, celebrity ownership, etc.

The reason for having to take these intangibles into consideration is due to a lack of relevant properties. After all, the term ultra-luxury implies a certain level of uniqueness that is beyond comparison. For example, to the average person a 1952 Mickey Mantle baseball card in mint condition is just a card made of glossed paper and ink, but to a card collector it is a piece of sports memorabilia with an exceptional history that is now worth around $30,000. This same rule applies to the pricing of high-end and ultra-luxury homes.

Furthermore, it is important to recognize that pricing is also a tool that determines how much effort, time, and money you, the agent, are willing to spend on marketing. In addition, pricing is the platform that determines risk levels and reward for the seller as well as for you. Keep in mind that mastering pricing in the luxury market is as important as understanding how to present a winning proposition to a bank in a short sale so the investor will accept a loss. Why the analogy? Many sellers in the luxury market do not need to sell and see the sale as a business transaction. Therefore, any listing presentation must have data to support the estimated value.

Determining the Core Value of a Property

To be viewed as an expert, the ability to provide value and depth of knowledge is the cornerstone for that distinction. The methodology for pricing luxury and ultra-luxury properties follows a different path from the traditional market. As I indicated earlier the value is created by being a true advisor, and advice must be provided with a superior level of detail to the seller as part of your value proposition. Years ago I learned the following formula from a friend who happens to be an appraiser:

> *Land + Replacement Cost – (Obsolescence and Age) + Amenities Value =*
> *Core Value of a Property*

Put on your professor glasses as I provide a brief explanation of the factors to consider:

- Land – What is the value of the land without any improvements? If there are any lots available, what have they sold for (not the listing price)? Since most high-net-worth individuals value privacy, what level of privacy does the property provide? Estimate the land value based on a judgment of the highest and best use of the land.

- Replacement Cost – Determine the cost of building a luxury property per square foot in your market. If you do not know ask two to three builders in your circle of influence or ask homeowners who recently had their property built. Another way is by identifying new construction in your area. Multiply the cost per square foot by the square footage of the subject property to get the estimated value of the replacement cost.

- Obsolescence and Age – There is a concept used by appraisers called "effective age" which differs from the actual age of the home. It is based on the amount of observed deterioration and obsolescence a home has sustained. In principle the level of maintenance or lack of it by its occupants influences the effective age of a home.

- Amenities Value – Your subject home may have a rare outdoor spa or a shooting range which other homes do not have. As with all adjustments, establish a value based on your knowledge of the market. There is no need to bother with exactitude since the value is subjective. At the end you will discuss it with the seller.

Other factors that affect the value of the property and must be considered:

- Functional Obsolescence – In reality functional obsolescence is not restricted to extremely old homes. The styles and tastes in America can change dramatically in as little as a decade. For example, an original house from the 1940s or 1950s may have tiny closets by today's standards. Another example in Florida is ceiling height; there is no such thing as a luxury home with 8.5-foot ceilings.

- Celebrity Value – Some buyers pay more for a home that was previously owned by a celebrity. This allows them to say, "The property was owned by so and so." This can be tricky as you will also attract people who just want to see the property, and even steal from the property just to have something their idol owned. Casa Casuarina is an example of a home that attracted the rich and famous to make a bid. A mansion in South Beach, Florida, which was the former home of Gianni Versace, sold for $41.5 million to the Nakash family that started Jordache Jeans. The Nakash family outbid the likes of the Gindi family of Century 21 department stores and Donald Trump in 2013 due to the uniqueness and celebrity status.

I stated that it isn't as simple as getting the seller to list with you and putting a big wooden sign on the lawn with your name on it, didn't I? As in any profession, not all professionals are alike. The successful realtor adds value through their ability to identify the unique traits of the property coupled with their expertise to assess the neighborhood, surrounding areas, and trends to quantify the value of the property. In addition, they have a keen ability to identify the best possible buyer.

Let's look at it in more detail. Real estate is always local and what is seen as a positive factor in one market may be negative in another market. Therefore, once you have a range of the core value of a property defined, compare it to other properties sold. Even though there may not be any similar property, keeping a list of what has sold in the luxury market in your area may help your client put the value of the home into perspective. It also shows the seller that you specialize in that particular market and sets you apart from the average commodity agent.

Presenting a Pricing Strategy to Achieve Win-Win-Win

In my opinion this is no different than preparing a presentation to a board of directors to sell services or a job interview. Therefore, I believe the preparation for the presentation should not be taken lightly. I indicated earlier that there is a lot of work involved. I also indicated that if you are an agent, you must collect all types of relevant data, analyze it, and be prepared to use it as supporting information. Understanding the audience and the uniqueness of a home have proved to be beneficial when working with clients. Make sure to highlight the key points you want to get across. The listing presentation is not a rehearsal.

In the traditional market prepare a one-page summary and a detailed competitive market analysis (CMA) based on comparable properties. Make sure you share the process with the seller so they are with you every step of the way. But do so in a concise and easy manner. Make sure the sellers are aware that there might be some fine-tuning since pricing is not an exact science and the market will show if the price is right on or not. For example, I just recently sold a house in less than 24 hours. The owners had contacted me three years earlier. At the time I explained why they would not get their price. I even suggested waiting a couple of years for the market to turn around.

Also be ready to share your marketing strategy with the seller as part of your presentation. Educate the seller and set expectations. I find that it is not about the real estate I am selling, but more about the people. It is important to share, with the exception of investors, that the majority of homebuyers are people who seek a narrative with the home. The copywriter on your team will be able to put together the narrative needed to attract buyers. Always remember that while part of that narrative is the pricing, the person must fall in love with the house like they fell in love with their high school sweetheart. As previously mentioned, to achieve my win with the seller I base my pricing recommendations on specific information about the property, but to achieve my win with the buyer, I support my value proposition to the buyer or buyer's agent with a narrative that makes them fall in love with the home.

When dealing with high-net-worth individuals, the rules change a bit. Since they are used to hiring experts in every field, you want to demonstrate your expertise and show your worth so they trust you. I recommend you provide a one page executive summary with your CMA. The CMA must include detailed, supporting evidence with a clear rationale of assumptions made regarding each component of the property and the rationale for the value of conclusion. Keep in mind they are looking for the rationale and the depth of examination of data behind it. However, sometimes there is more to it than simple expertise. I once had a seller who almost didn't work with me because he didn't know me, but I knew a friend of his. He took a chance and gave me his listing. Not only did I sell that property, I sold it for a price that he didn't think was possible. That same seller then gave me another listing and when I sold that one for the highest price ever in the neighborhood, he began to call me his "hustler realtor" and spoke to friends and family about using my services. I became his go-to realtor as he likes "hustlers." I demonstrated my expertise and I asserted myself in a way that ensured a cultivation of constant business.

We Are a Global Market

I have always been fascinated by other cultures and faraway places. In the early '90s, I remember telling my ex-husband that someday I would combine this interest with my technology background to work internationally. And I did in 1993 while still working at Digital Equipment Corporation. How could I forget that promise? What I never anticipated was that the knowledge I accumulated during my international stint would be useful in the real estate industry. All those years of heavy travel and being away from my family gave me a great understanding of business culture. For example, if I am dealing with a Chinese businessperson, I am well aware of the "Saving Face" concept, in addition to understanding I must hold a business card with my two hands, look at it, and not even think of writing on it.

Regardless if you are fascinated by other cultures like me or not, technology has facilitated the phenomenon of globalization that we enjoy today; social media is one of those enabler platforms. No matter where you live in the US, someone who lives in another part of the world could be the prospective buyer of your home. For example, I remember when wealthy individuals from Venezuela would come to buy property in the US because of our stability during Hugo Chávez's reign and after his death. There was a fear of instability in Venezuela, and those with means saw the US real estate market as a stable place to put their money. What about people from China? Did you know that the Chinese have surpassed Canadians when it comes to purchasing real estate in the US? Also consider this: the average home purchased by buyers from China is over $800,000. And the best part of dealing with Chinese buyers is they tend to purchase their homes in cash. There are few things professionally sweeter than having a sale of a $800,000 home close in less than a month because the buyer brought a check with them.

It is imperative to recognize the rise of developing economies across the globe coincides with a similar expansion of housing markets needs. Furthermore, as wealth becomes more available to new members of the middle class, more people will want to purchase new homes and benefit from the strategies other wealthy individuals have used. Can you blame them? Owning your home isn't an exclusively American dream. Owning a home brings status, a place that is uniquely yours, and a possible investment opportunity. People here in the US buy homes with the intention of holding them as investments and the same is true for buyers from around the world. Buying a home is the preferred investment not only because of the safety and stability that often comes from the market, but also because of the potential for value appreciation and a hedge against inflation and currency fluctuations, according to the Association of Foreign Investors in Real Estate.[1] One need only look at the current political strife between the US, Europe, and Russia. Ever since the United Nations placed economic sanctions on Russia, we have seen a greater than average flow of Russian investors buying real estate in the US. Do you think they do so because they love the sunny beaches of Miami or the famous Broadway shows of New York? Not entirely. They purchase real estate in the US because they know that there is a finite amount of land and purchasing it in the US is a stable, constant, and secure investment that, with the exception of the housing bubble of 2007, often provides the best opportunity for capital appreciation.

The emergence of globalization is another reason to hire a realtor who is creative and knows how to market your home directly to the people who would be a perfect fit for that type of property, regardless of their location in the world. To that perfect fit buyer, the price of the home can become a sticker they simply look at. A person at a three-star Michelin restaurant will not argue over the price of the food and neither will the buyer of your home so long as you market it perfectly to them. That marketing begins by doing it with the right digital age mindset.

Marketing Homes in the Digital Age

As you probably already noticed, the years of selling real estate by just putting a sign in the front yard and placing the listing on the MLS are long gone, unless you expect your buyer to be one of the neighbors. Furthermore, if you think that just because your home is listed on the MLS it will sell itself, you're wrong. Therefore, regardless of the type of property, it is important to recognize

---

[1]   "D.C. Real Estate Continues Steady Decline Among Foreign Investors as N.Y. Deposes London as Top Global City," *2015 AFIRE Annual Foreign Investment Survey* (January 5, 2015), http://afire.membership-software.org/files/Final%20Main%20Press%20Release(1).docx

that even though we live in a global market, you have to recognize that it is about the right combination of direct target marketing campaigns, both online and offline. Global marketing is even more prevalent in the luxury market. According to Laurie Moore-Moore, founder of the Institute for Luxury Home Marketing in Dallas, Texas, "What sets the sales of luxury homes apart is that each property requires its own marketing plan and likely the home will be bought by an out-of-state buyer. And, the more expensive the home, the more likely the buyer will come from more than 500 miles away."[2] And as an expert and member of the Institute for Luxury Home Marketing I know that agents with this knowledge recognize there is a significant marketing investment required to successfully sell a luxury property. These agents are also aware this investment will net seven to ten times the cash invested because it has less Days on Market and a higher sale price.

As indicated earlier, I have broken the price record in a community by identifying the characteristics of the potential buyer based on the list of unique amenities of the home. I knew these amenities were important to that potential buyer and used them to formulate a marketing campaign geared toward people who would be a perfect fit for that type of home. This approach placed the property in front of the best candidates to purchase it based on similar interests. The key is to describe as much as possible to the perfect buyer. Does the home have a four-car garage with car lifts? Target a car enthusiast who has, or might be starting, a car collection. Market directly to them and they will pay market value if the need is there. By the way, it could well be that the buyer was not looking to buy, but when presented with a property that they have an interest in, they will consider its purchase. This no different than when you go shopping and stumble upon something you must have. Window displays of a property work just as well as a window display for the latest DKNY or Chanel fashion. Know your buyer and show them what they are missing and must have.

---

[2]   Jane Hodges, "How High-End Brokers Market Luxury Homes", The Wall Street Journal (*July 22, 2004*), http://www.wsj.com/articles/SB126289221288120125

That is the beauty of direct target marketing; it is all about identifying the amenities and the audience to go after.

The Internet Is Not a "Thing"; It's the New Reality

We have lived in a world driven by technology since the '90s. I will never forget the first time I accessed the Internet in 1986. I had just started working for Digital Equipment Corporation after graduating from college and I never imagined the Internet would change the world like it did. Because of the Internet and social media, consumers of both million dollar and mass market homes are surfing Realtor.com, Redfin, Trulia, and Zillow, among other real estate listing websites, to find a home. They browse through many properties even before they call an agent. The photos of the properties, virtual tours and information posted serve as a qualification tool.

Another tool is e-blast marketing to the local and non-local brokerage community. E-blasts should be part of the marketing strategy because no stone should be left unturned. I still use the established methods because agents are working with the buyers who may be the perfect candidate to purchase the property. But for the most part, today's buyers are savvy and use the Internet to boost their buying capability. Like a fish drawn to the hook, you need the bait to reel them in. If marketing both offline and using the latest technology online catch a buyer's interest like the bait on a fishing rod, staging a home is the hook around that bait that will ensure you reel in the purchaser.

Getting the Home Ready for the Photo Shoot

With every high-end market listing, at a minimum, I insist that we stage the home and have professional photos taken to present the property in its best light. I also hire a copywriter to work with me to create a stellar brochure that highlights the home's best features. These steps set the foundation to procure the highest price.

I love reading every interior design magazine that I can get my hands on and I have always enjoyed helping friends decorate their homes. So helping my clients stage their home for a Luxury sale has become a natural component of my marketing strategy. I have been able to help clients stage their homes for sales that have resulted in the best and highest prices possible. Whether a short sale, traditional resale, or Luxury resale, the goal is the same: to highlight the property's positive aspects.

Staging displays the home's potential and provides prospective buyers with a sense of what's possible. The goal is to evoke a cozy and inviting feeling as well as highlight the best features of the property. Staging can get expensive, so on various occasions I've found some creative ways to stretch a dollar for maximum impact. First we clean the home, mow the lawn, and then we declutter it by removing all the items that make the home appear disheveled. Displaying all your family photos is important and I get it, but displaying forty-one pictures of your child's wisdom tooth removal by the entrance to the kitchen makes it difficult for potential buyers to see themselves living in the property. Next, I go through the closets and make sure all the items are neatly folded and well organized. The rooms need to have balance and flow. We move furniture and accessories to provide the right ambiance to potential buyers so they can see themselves living the lifestyle the home affords.

However, sometimes sellers want to create their own ambiance in ways that hamper what you're trying to achieve. On one occasion when I was invited by the owner into his residence, the first thing I noticed was a lack of softness to the home. The townhouse was a symphony of battleship gray walls, low-lit walkways, rooms full of boxes, and it had artificial plants that looked like they had been collecting dust for years hanging everywhere. While some buyers may be single men, the majority of homebuyers in that particular neighborhood were families. When I told the owner that he needed to buy new high-output lights, he looked uneasy but accepted my recommendation. Unfortunately, the moment I suggested that he soften the home to attract women, he responded, "That's why I have silk plants. Women love hanging, fake plants!"

Here is a tip for any guy who happens to be reading this book—fake plants do not attract women, they just attract dust. Besides, they show you are incapable of caring for live plants. Here is another tip—if you have live plants, make sure they are green and healthy. There is nothing worse than plants that are brown and wilted. Fake plants with years of accumulated dust fare better than dead plants, but just. In fact, if you aren't sure about your ability to keep any plant alive for more than a week, just keep the walls clean without anything hanging. You'll thank me for it.

On the flip side, some homeowners are creative and share ideas they saw on *Property Brothers* on HGTV. I can sense, for that moment at least, the homeowner is having fun. Remember that staging a home is like preparing for a first date; the first impression you give your date is what can make or break the date, and staging a home is no different.

Like a First Date, Your House Makes a Lasting Impression

If you ask me about the first date I had with my ex-husband or with my significant other, I can tell you quite a few details and the feelings that went through my veins. That is because each one of us can remember important milestones in our lives: the first kiss, the first baseball game, the first car, and the list goes on. The first time people see their dream home is no different. For that reason you need to treat how people see your home the way you would prepare for a date. First impressions last longer than you would imagine.

A good example of this is my son's apartment during law school. For the record, I adore my son, but he will be the first to admit that his sense of style is more "Downton Abbey" than Ellie Cullman's "modern traditional" and aesthetic design. In other words, not so trendy. When he found a place that he loved I went to visit him with a plan to make his apartment stylish, hoping that he would get out of his Victorian era preferences. That very weekend I made sure that we bought furniture, portraits, plates, and other home décor that exemplified a more modern version of his persona. Like most of my clients, my son huffed and puffed and threatened to blow the house down, while complaining, "Mom, I'm in law school, I don't need this stuff." I ignored his complaints because I know that he likes to entertain people. Eventually my son got into the shopping mode and we had fun. Two weeks later he called to share that he had a housewarming party with some of his law school classmates. He told me that his female classmates in particular liked the apartment. To make a long story short, he likes to joke that our "apartment makeover" was part of his dating strategy. It seems that he has moved toward a more transitional style. Like I said, you dress to impress on a first date, and a home's first impression can make or break a sale.

Staging: Another Must!

Barbara Corcoran said, "The advent of the internet set the stage for home staging; without the home staged people would not come to see the house." In an interview with the CEO of Real Estate Staging Association, Shell Broadnax. Barbara also added, "It used to be an extra and now is essential"[3] I completely agree with her because I have seen what it has done for some of my listings. I have used physical staging as well as virtual staging. Either of those two approaches, when aesthetically created, brings exceptional results. I recently sold a $1.3 million dollar property where one of the rooms was originally empty. I have found that only a small percentage of homebuyers can visualize the potential of a vacant home, therefore, I virtually staged the room. The room looked amazing and gave people ideas. It was a minimum investment. When a house is staged it can make a great difference in selling dollars. Therefore, I often recommend that if nothing else can be done to stage the home, at least paint the interior.

3 Shell Brodnax, "Interview with Barbara Corcoran from ABC's Shark Tank", Real Estate Staging Association (*Feb 12, 2014*), http://www.realestatestagingassociation.com/content.aspx?page_id=22&club_id=304550&module_id=196601

Especially if the current colors are out-of-date or the walls have lots of marks. A good paint resurfacing can make a huge difference. Plus, the smell of fresh paint makes the home seem newer. For example, I listed an investment property that was getting plenty of offers in the $450,000 range, but this was far less than the fair market value and much less than the net proceeds the bank was willing to accept to approve the short sale. I was fortunate to have a cooperative seller who invested resources in painting the interior and cleaning up loose cables and other debris. As part of my marketing strategy, I staged the home virtually—using photography and Photoshop to insert décor for a stunning visual effect. Additionally, I hired a company that creates a virtual tour video complete with mood music that showed the property at its best. The video was convincing. No one would ever know the home was virtually staged.

> Staging is a strategic decision and also an investment to highlight the best features a home has to offer to the most opportune buyer. It is definitely an alternative to having to lower the price of a home.

For added effect, I blew up still photos from the video and placed them on easels in each room in the home so when potential buyers came for a showing, they could connect the property to what they saw in the video. This marketing approach was sensational. It created such a demand that the residence went under contract for $719,000 in the first weekend. There are various companies today that provide this service. You can see some examples of staged rooms on the following websites:

- http://www.hasten.me
- http://www.virtualstagingllc.com
- http://virtuallystagingproperties.com

Figure 2 shows before and after photos of a bedroom and a living room virtually staged.

Virtual staging and visualization provided by Leonard Minsky, CEO of Hasten Inc.

A homeowner approached me to sell their house. The house had a lovely, manicured front yard. The doors looked like I was walking into a medieval castle, which was a slight cause for concern, but it was the inside of the home that truly shocked me. Once inside the home, I walked into the kitchen and could not believe what I saw in front of my eyes—lime green cabinets. As I began taking notes, I realized the living room color scheme was purple, turquoise, and more lime green. That is when I asked, "What are you planning to do with the house?" To which the homeowners replied, "Well, we are planning to get new wood cabinets for the kitchen." I immediately asked, "What about the rest of the house?" Without any delay the husband replied, "Nothing." I knew then that I needed to see the rest of the house to assess what needed to be done if I was going to take the listing to sell the house.

In the master bedroom the bed hung from metal chains and the master bath had an array of oranges and reds. To my surprise, each room differed in color, from purple to yellow to green to black.

I immediately had a flashback to a previous client; remember that house I told you about with the perfume collection? Visions of constant list price drops swirled in my head unless I corrected this client's expectations for a sale. I took the opportunity to share the previously mentioned incident with my clients and explained that finding someone who would fall in love with the house the way it was and pay prime dollars would be almost impossible.

After convincing them to remove some of the art from the walls, repaint all the walls of the house to neutral colors, put the hanging bed on the ground, and cover the metal hooks with a big comforter in the master bedroom, the owners further followed my instructions by paying for trendy staging pieces. What could have been a difficult sale, and perhaps a short sale on the low end of the neighborhood, ended up selling for the highest price in the area over an eighteen month period, prompting other realtors to stage their homes similarly to try and upstage that sale! My client became a believer and was thrilled with the outcome.

Showings: Time to Get the House on the Real Estate Stage

Once we have set the asking price, listed the property, staged it, and completed the marketing, it's time to bring people in and let the showings begin. I find the best-case scenario is to create anticipation around the property and the showing. One great strategy for this is to hold an open house, but not just any open house. I like to promote the home, without allowing anyone to see it before the open house. When the property is in great condition—or even in good condition and in a great location—people will often start bidding on it even if they haven't seen it, just to try to get in ahead of the crowd.

If the property is in less than average condition, I explain to the seller that we need to do as many showings as possible to make the home available and take every appointment that comes. This is for two reasons. First, one man's trash is another man's treasure, and by showing it as many times as possible, you are more likely to hit upon that man who sees the treasure. Second, if the house stays on the market for longer than average, it can create a stigma attached to the listing. It is not unheard of for other agents to call a listing agent and the first thing they ask is, "What's wrong with the house? Why hasn't it sold yet?" Buyer's agents are inquisitive by nature and they assess how to get the best deal possible for their clients, which is why several buyers' agents hate it when I revert to my Corporate America ways and keep a tight lid on what information I give freely. The main thing is exposure. Under certain circumstances it is a numbers game—the more people, the better the chance of procuring a buyer, as opposed to specifically targeting the most opportune buyers. I remember selling a house that smelled like dog urine and it clearly had a moldy odor throughout. Despite this the homeowner was adamant that their property was the best house in the neighborhood and that showings should be restricted to a narrow time frame and only for buyers who had to meet stringent qualification criteria. After receiving nothing but insultingly lowball offers, I explained that to get a buyer the property needed to be shown as many times as possible. Once the seller relaxed his criteria, we eventually found a buyer who made an offer close to the listing price.

I never recommend private showings unless the prospect has their realtor in attendance or I have another person accompany me to the showing. In the high-end market especially, some shady characters with criminal intentions contact the listing agent directly and pose as buyers. They may be previewing the property for the purpose of planning a later criminal act or worse, attack the realtor. I make safety part of my business strategy.

With regards to scheduling showings, the easiest way to show a property is when it is vacant, as opposed to when it is occupied. Scheduling showings around clients' schedules can be the biggest challenge. I've had several cases where the family did not want the home shown when the kids were present for fear it would upset them. I also have had elderly or severely depressed homeowners who could only tolerate one showing a day or just a few times a week. And of course, working with tenants can present a host of challenges.

Some tenants are flexible about scheduling while others will try to sabotage the sale during the showings so they can remain in the home longer. I had one instance where the tenant was so committed to staying that during every showing they would tell prospective buyers what a terrible property it was. I had another who would only allow showings for one hour from Monday through Thursday, and to make matters worse, she would remind the potential buyer when their hour was up. I vividly remember one tenant who, when the buyers were on their way out with their realtor, called them back into the house to see the septic tank overflowing. We learned later the tenant had stuffed some towels into the pipes to manufacture the overflow. Ultimately, I had to attend every showing to keep the tenant quiet. I knew she wouldn't dare spin these lies while I was present. Each one of these listings sold, but the aggravation and time spent dealing with these tenants was, to put it politely, *memorable*. Again, my suggestion is to give the tenant an incentive to cooperate before you start scheduling showings.

Conclusion

The most successful negotiations are those where each party leaves the table feeling they gained something from the transaction. Real estate may be a contact sport, but not a blood sport. A bad taste in a buyer's or seller's mouth can lead to trouble in unexpected ways, so try to understand each side's motivations. Whether you are an agent, buyer, or seller, the key to win-win-win is achieved by making sure the interests of the other parties are addressed. Just remember it is not always about price; it could be as simple as the buyer's need to close by a certain date because their kids will be attending school in the fall and they want to move in before school starts. Or as in my personal situation, I did not want to sell my home until my son graduated from college and left for law school. So once you identify those needs or wants, find an effective way to satisfy other individual's interests while meeting yours. After all, that is how the win-win-win can be achieved.

"Nothing is predestined. The obstacles of your past can become the gateways that lead to new beginnings."

—Ralph Blum

5

Short Sales Come in Different Sizes

Real estate is one of those industries where we can succeed or fail regardless of our finances, education, or background. Any investment in one's own home can swing like a pendulum, bountiful one moment, but when it swings the other way it could be terrifying. I have chosen two stories to illustrate this. One is a story of a timber tycoon losing millions. The other one is my story.

Not Your Average Short Sale

In 1982, Mr. John Rudey purchased a fifty-one acre estate known as Copper Beech Farm, named after the large copper beech trees populating the property in Greenwich, Connecticut. On April 11, 2014, the twelve-bedroom waterfront mansion was sold for $120 million, making the real estate transaction the most expensive home sold in United States history at the time, according to *Forbes Magazine.*[4] What you probably don't know is the signifi-

---

[4]   Erin Carlyle, "Most Expensive U.S. Home Sale Ever: Connecticut Estate Goes For $120 Million", *Forbes* (April 16, 2014), http://www. forbes.com/sites/erincarlyle/2014/04/16/copper-beech-farm-for-120-million-is-americas-new-most-expensive-home-sale/.

cance of this sale. This sale represented the most expensive short sale. And yes, you read that right, *the most expensive short sale.*

Copper Beech Farm features a 75-foot pool, grass tennis courts, and a stone carriage house. Wild turkeys regularly roam the estate along an 1,800-foot-long driveway that meanders up to the main house. The mansion has fifteen thousand square feet of living space and an additional seven thousand square feet of basement and attic space.

The waterfront property once belonged to Andrew Carnegie's niece, Harriet Lauder Greenway, whose father, George Lauder, co-founded the venture that eventually became US Steel. The mansion was built in 1896 with Victorian and French Renaissance influences on an estate with four thousand feet of private frontage on Long Island Sound, and it includes a pair of offshore islands.

When initially purchased in 1982, the property quietly sold for $7.55 million. It might seem hard to imagine how Mr. Rudey found himself in financial trouble serious enough to put him in a position where he was faced with a possible foreclosure. Even though his story is no different than the story of many high-net-worth homeowners, its scale was much larger.

From time to time, Mr. Rudey needed cash to cover excess expenses for some of his business misfortunes. In 2006, he refinanced the estate with a $59 million mortgage through Bank of America, which was personally guaranteed by both Mr. and Mrs. Rudey. It was around that time that Mr. Rudey's timber companies started to hit great difficulties, and later that year, another one of his companies went bankrupt in Oregon.

Then, at the end of 2010, he cross-collateralized the $59 million mortgage on Copper Beech with a $79 million mortgage on his Washington forestland. Both loans were with Bank of America. In addition to that mortgage, he had $65 million in mortgages on another part of Copper Beech through M&T Bank, bringing the total debt on the estate to $203 million. This meant that if the Rudeys fell behind on any payments, any one of the banks could foreclose. The Rudeys defaulted.

By 2011, foreclosure proceedings on the Bank of America portion of Copper Beech started, and the Rudeys filed a suit against the bank claiming "predatory lending practices." The following summer they dropped the lawsuit and listed the property.

Although the final price was shy of its original asking price of $190 million, this sale is exceptionally notable for what it represents—an excellent example of how high-net-worth homeowners have encountered economic hardship yet avoided foreclosure, protected their assets, and regained their freedom through a well-executed short sale.

What most people in the middle of financial hardship do not realize is that they have the ability to regain their freedom. This financial freedom is not exclusive to high-net-worth homeowners. It is available to those who are willing to make the difficult first step. It happened to a middle class father whose wife left him with two kids. That single father has found a wonderful girlfriend and they are planning to buy their next home together. This freedom can even happen to a single mother trying to help her son go through college.

> Copper Beech Farm sold for $120 million in Greenwich, CT on April 11, 2014. It is the most notable short sale. And, at the time it was America's most expensive home sold.

Short Sales Happen

I won't ever forget that dreadful call. I should have felt an ominous premonition as it began to rain earlier that afternoon. I could feel my hands sweating as I dialed the number of the bank. I started to drink a cup of green tea to calm me down. It was so hard to get the words out of my mouth, but I kept saying to myself, "I have dealt with difficult situations in the past, I can do it."

Then as soon as the bank representative went through her routine disclosures, I started to pour my heart out, "I lost my job last year due to a company restructuring and I have exhausted my savings and retirement money. Is there anything the bank can do to help me keep my home?"

She responded as if waiting for this moment, "Sell your furniture and if you still can't make your payments, sell your belongings. You have jewelry and valuables, right? Sell them so you can make your mortgage payments. I just can't help you until you become current on your payments, and maybe we can do something later."

Suddenly, like a death sentence given by an unsympathetic judge from a TV drama, I could feel the walls close around me while I made a last attempt to gain the bank representative's understanding. I asked, "You are telling me that I have to sell my furniture and everything valuable? What happens after that?"

I understood that the woman on the phone worked for a financial institution and that after speaking with so many people in a similar situation, she had become immune to people in my situation. But I kept thinking how was I supposed to become current on my payments if I was behind by three months and I had no money left. Perhaps she misunderstood my situation, so I responded, "Ms. White, I just told you, I have used all my savings and I have almost no IRA money left. Is there anything the bank can do?"

Her immediate response was, "That's your fault, you should have thought of that." Even the tone of her voice suggested a feeling of disgust. At this point, the taste of my green tee became especially bitter with every sip I took.

I stopped and caught my breath and responded, "But I have worked so hard and tried every single avenue!" No matter what I said there was nothing that was going to change her mind. All I could think of were the facts in front of me—that I had been laid off in the worst recession since the Great Depression and I had burned through my entire savings, retirement accounts, etc.

"Why don't you get a regular job?" she inquired as she made it sound as if I had not tried hard enough and I was less of a person for getting into this situation.

"But I've looked extensively, Ms. White," I replied. "Humph," I heard over the line once I finished pouring my troubles out to her.

"So you can't find a job to even pay your mortgage?" To which I responded, "I have been profusely looking for one." I could not believe that Ms. White did not want to hear anything I was confessing. I knew I had failed, I was disappointed with myself, and it was hard to admit my failure to anyone. Nevertheless, Ms. White asked again, "You have furniture, right?" "Yes," I responded, confused by her inquisition. "Well like I told you earlier, the only solution you have is to sell your furniture and valuables to make your mortgage current. You just don't qualify for anything and you need to make your payments."

Looking back, I understand that was her job, but that was my home and she was dissecting an extension of me in such an insensitive way that it compounded the pain and anguish I was enduring.

The Journey Home

During the earlier part of my adult life, I moved almost every two years because of job relocations. I have had people like Muhammad Ali, with whom I shared great conversations on various summer afternoons back in the '70s, as a neighbor. I have a lot of things to thank him for, but that is not the topic of this book. I have also been fortunate to live in neighborhoods with people like Danny White from the Dallas Cowboys, Rubén Sierra, the All-Star baseball player, and Bernie Parmalee from the Miami Dolphins. And I must admit that even though it was nice to live with "the rich and famous," as Robin Leach would put it, nothing compared to the feeling of buying my home. Sure, I bought a home for the first time when I was nineteen, but that was with my ex-husband. The feeling of buying a home all on my own compared to the first kiss I ever had. I felt like a caterpillar coming out of its cocoon. It was life changing. That home was a symbol of me and my achievements. That is probably the reason I tried to hold on to it for as long as I could.

I remember the day we moved into the house. My son's friends had all come to help us move and all I could think of was how fortunate I was to be able to provide for my son and me. It was just like I had always dreamed.

After all, I earned my Bachelor's degree in Computer Science and worked in information technology because I wanted to make sure I could provide for my family if needed and at that moment, I was. At that time I was proud of my accomplishments. I could remember after getting my degree I went to work in technology and how I rose through the corporate ranks.

Unexpectedly, at the peak of the Great Recession, I was "downsized." After a few days reality set in. I had lost my job. I was so afraid to lose everything. Unfortunately, the first time I had lost a job was right after my divorce and the fears were overwhelming. But this time there was something different and I knew it; my head was in the right place. And even though my head was in the right place, I had grown up in such a sheltered way that I was not aware that my Pollyanna attitude would serve as a blind spot in spite of graduating at the top of my class from college.

I tried to build my own business. When that did not work, I immediately set out to find another job. Despite my arduous efforts, a year passed and I had yet to find a suitable position. I had been living off my savings and my cash reserve was running low. Then real estate prices plunged even further, and all of a sudden, my "great investment" had turned into my greatest liability. I couldn't afford to keep my home, yet my heart wouldn't let me give it up. What a dilemma!

I won't lie, I cried a lot. I had not felt this defeated since my divorce. The feelings of shame were overwhelming to the point that I did not tell any of my friends or my family what I was going through. I had let myself and my son down.

I have gone through various challenges—just like others—but next to my divorce and watching my son leave to serve in Iraq as an Army medic, letting my home go was the hardest thing I have ever had to come to terms with. No matter how hard I had worked or how many successes I'd had throughout my career, I felt like a failure.

Suddenly, I looked outside my window and decided to come up with the courage to move on. I finally realized I had to let go. Like a tumor or a cyst, it had to be removed. It might leave a scar, but I had to do what was necessary to survive.

Light at the End of the Tunnel

The day I made the decision to move forward, the beginning of my future started to take shape. I embarked on my journey with the firm belief that there was no turning back. And even though I knew nothing about the real estate industry, I decided to conquer it; I knew that it had to be done. Like the British facing down the whole of occupied Europe at the start of WWII—they didn't know how they would do it, but they knew it had to be won. The Great Recession, the worst since the Great Depression, was in full swing and I had been a casualty of that crisis. I swore I would help others who were caught in its clutches and like me, were willing to move forward and not become victims.

Once I made that decision, it made it easier to release the feelings of defeat and shame attached to my mortgage failure. Instead, I embraced the opportunity to move forward. I started to view the short sale process for what it was, just an exit strategy.

A year after this difficult moment in my life, I passed my real estate exam. Two weeks later I found a broker to work under and a lawyer who was willing to review every single listing and sale's offer I received.

Ever since that day I understood real estate in a different way. It is not about the sale transaction. It is about emotions, family, identity, and finding a place that reflects you. As for me, I found the one thing; I found myself in essence and purpose.

In my world today, I like to see myself as a catalyst of change whether I take the role of someone who helps her clients move to the next step in life to avoid foreclosure or grow their financial investments. Regardless of the transaction or the client I know it is all about them. I see myself as someone who has gone through a journey similar to my clients. Experiencing a short sale was a liberating experience because it helped me stand by my convictions and act in spite of fears. And most important, it provided a different perspective that gives me an edge when working with people who, like me, were forced to surrender control and let their home go. After all, you still have you, and I can honestly say there is light at the end of the tunnel.

Thought Provoking Questions for Those Considering a Short Sale

1. What was the most difficult financial time or life-changing circumstance you have ever had? Did you overcome it or freeze on the spot?

2. If you had to move and sell your home what is the one step you would take today?

3. If you've had to sell your home how did you feel afterward?

4. If similar circumstances arise what could you do differently?

5. What could you do to prevent them from reoccurring?

Thought Provoking Questions for Those Looking from the Outside

1. Are you like the man I wrote about in the preface in the navy blue suit with a red handkerchief judging others' misfortunes?

2. Do you believe that foreclosure is a lower socioeconomic issue?

3. Do you believe that people who decide to do a short sale are avoiding responsibility or looking for an easy way out?

4. Under difficult circumstances are you the friend or the judge?

If you answered yes to either 2 or 3, think of the $120 million dollar short sale. Mr. Rudey had to make a difficult decision, no different than most people who have been faced with it. The only difference is the size of the loss.

"When one door closes another door opens,
but we so often look so long and so regretfully
upon the closed door, that we do not see
the ones which open for us."

—Alexander Graham Bell

6

The Property ISN'T Distressed in a Short Sale, the Homeowner Is

The real estate industry uses the term "distressed" to refer to a property where the owner is delinquent on their mortgage payments. A home occupied by people who can't pay the mortgage often shows the symptoms of poor upkeep that go hand in hand with the inability to pay the debt service.

But in a luxury short sale, the literal definition doesn't necessarily mean the property is in disrepair. In fact, of the properties I've facilitated through short sales, about half showed no outward signs of distress at all. And even if the property shows signs of wear, it is still a rare jewel in a great neighborhood, and a few low-cost repairs together with creative staging can make the property as desirable as ever.

I worked with a client who had two investment properties with underwater mortgages. In this instance, one of the properties was in disrepair. We staged the clean property while the other was left unfinished due to economic difficulties. Getting both of the properties under contract was easy. Unfortunately, the contract on the property that was in disrepair fell through and that is when the problems began.

After the contract fell through, I was only able to get offers of fifteen percent below the minimum amount requested by the lender to approve the short sale. After a few months of trying unsuccessfully to help my client get a better offer, I convinced my client to partially stage the property. A week after a nominal investment of under $10,000 we received an offer at list price and the lender approved the short sale. The money spent was a minor investment compared to the benefit of obtaining a waiver of the deficiency. We went to settlement on both properties and my client was relieved of any deficiency on both properties.

In the luxury market it is vital that the realtor and the homeowner both view the property in the highest regard. The fact that the real estate property is being offered as a short sale should not be an excuse to treat the advertising, marketing, and showing of the luxury home as any less than the gem that it is. Any A-quality house in A-quality condition in an A-quality location will do well if advertised, marketed, staged, and priced correctly. If the house is in C-condition but located in an A-quality location and resources are limited, then the realtor you select for your listing must be creative and talented enough to do whatever is needed to present the property in the best light to attract viable buyers at the highest price possible. Otherwise, the bank is less likely to approve the short sale without requiring a promissory note to make up a portion of the deficiency.

Remember, at the end of it all, you are asking an investor who initially put down real money to take a loss. The goal of the realtor and seller should be to satisfactorily mitigate that loss. This is the only certain way to walk away with the investor waiving the deficiency.

The First Steps—Engage Your Team

As soon as I start working with a new client, I walk them through a methodical process to provide a solid foundation from which to operate. This helps ensure we have everything lined up and minimizes the number of unpleasant surprises. In the years I have been doing luxury home sales and short sales, I find the best scenario involves a relentless, resilient homeowner who is serious about his or her desire to move forward and avoid foreclosure, combined with knowledgeable real estate agents, a cooperative lender, and an educated buyer. When these are all in place, the transaction can happen with grace.

Start with the Right Agent

It is important to remember that real estate agents have specialties like any other professional. If you need an attorney for a medical malpractice suit, you do not even think of hiring an attorney who specializes in maritime law. They are both attorneys, but each specializes in different fields, sometimes to the exclusion of all others. Using this same principle, why would anyone looking to secure a short sale hire a real estate professional with no experience in short sales?

Furthermore, people use the terms realtor and real estate agent loosely, but not every real estate agent is a realtor. Although both are licensed to sell real estate in a particular state, there is a difference—a real estate agent can only qualify as a realtor when that agent is a member of the National Association of Realtors. Furthermore, realtors subscribe to the Realtor Code of Ethics, while a real estate agent does not. The Realtor Code of Ethics prohibits an agent from working outside of the agent's specialty. Some agents may argue that experience in a particular neighborhood lays the groundwork for a specialty. However, the difference between a short sale and a traditional equity resale is too great to simply be separated by neighborhood, city, or county.

Anyone going through the foreclosure process or any buyer who desires to purchase a short sale should hire a real estate agent who not only *claims* to specialize in short sales, but can also demonstrate that he or she has successfully brought many to settlement. Unless the listing agent specializes in distressed properties, the skills or experience needed to successfully manage the short sale while helping the homeowners avoid foreclosure may not be present.

Some real estate agents have advanced their knowledge by training to become certified as either a Certified Distressed

Property Expert (CDPE) or by completing the Short Sales and Foreclosure Resource Certification (SFR), or both. The initial training for CDPE and/or SFR provides the framework for understanding how to negotiate with lenders and how to qualify committed buyers. Agents with any of these certifications have the know-how to identify sellers who genuinely want to move forward with their lives.

For me, gaining fundamental short sale knowledge was the first requirement, but it was not enough. Due to my commitment to being a luxury short sale expert, in addition to becoming a certified CDPE, I earned the Certified Luxury Home Marketing Specialist (CLHMS) designation. I emphasize the word "earned" because realtors who hold the CLHMS designation have documented closed sales of homes priced in the top ten percent of residential real estate in their markets. Look for a realtor with the pedigree that combines general knowledge with specific luxury short sale experience.

It is similar to a surgeon who goes through a residency to obtain experience in one area of specialization. I understand that some people will place a surgeon's preparation in higher regard than a realtor's, and I am absolutely not going to dispute that. But I can assure you that realtors with expertise in luxury short sales have a tremendous positive impact on their clients' lives. To be a catalyst in aiding my clients' ability to move forward is more gratifying than I ever dreamed.

It Takes a Team

Listing with an experienced realtor in high-end short sales is a great start because your realtor may assist you in navigating the maze of lenders' bureaucracies, coordinating other members of the team, setting clear expectations and timelines, handling the advertising, staging, showings and offers, and expediting lender approval before the closing deadline.

When building your team make sure you have the right key professionals on board. An attorney experienced in foreclosures, short sales, asset protection, and estate planning, as well as an accountant, must be part of that team. Even the best realtor can't interpret the law for you or give tax advice without being a lawyer and/or an accountant.

The most important reason for consulting with an attorney is the issue of confidentiality. Attorney-client privilege protects communications and consultations between homeowner and attorney. Conversations between homeowners and their realtor are not protected. For the reasons previously indicated, distressed high-net-worth homeowners must work closely with their team of professionals to get the added benefits of advice on legal ways to protect their assets and ways to strategize for worst-case scenarios before they arise. As the realtor I also like to meet with the attorney to make sure our actions are aligned.

Finally, an experienced title company/closing agent is critical. Many circumstances take place during the short sale process where the closing agent is a key team player. I will discuss this in more detail in a later chapter.

Time is of the Essence

When I consider taking on a new short sale client, the first question I ask is whether there is a "judicial sale" date or a "summary judgment" scheduled. Not intending any disrespect to my client, I double-check public records to make sure they gave me the correct date and that we have time to attempt the short sale. I have been able to process short sales and close within forty-five days, but it's not easy. Knowing this information in advance allows any listing agent to identify the type of buyer needed to close within an aggressive window of time.

If there are less than thirty days left to process the short sale before a foreclosure sale date, the top priority becomes going to the lender to seek a cancellation of the sale date. Alternatively, if the seller has an attorney, he or she can file for a cancellation of the sale date. Of course a cancellation of the sale date does not stop a foreclosure, but it can postpone it long enough to complete a short sale. The older the file the more difficult it is to get the court to cancel the sale date. But the key here is to alert the lender that we are pursuing a short sale and get them on board to complete the transaction.

There are times when the homeowner has come to the realization too late. I had clients who kept delaying the process by either not signing papers or returning them late. I had a couple that kept doing that until the bank's negotiator closed the file. At that time it was too late to start new negotiations. Explaining to my clients that they were going into foreclosure was heartbreaking. They pleaded with me to continue, telling me, "I'll send them everything they want, just don't let them take my home!" I understood where my clients were emotionally and I also understood that it was hard for them to let go, but they never fully understood the reality of the situation and were forced into foreclosure.

Will the Real Owner Please Stand Up?

Before I list a property, I check to see whose name is on the deed. I need to be sure that the people signing the listing agreement and subsequent documents are the people whose names are on the title and mortgage. Then I check to be sure everyone named on the title is alive. If it turns out one of them is deceased, I need to understand what effect that has on the title. This is one of those times in the process where it is important to have a good working relationship with the title company or closing agent. In addition, if one or all of the owners on the title have died, I make a note to be ready to provide a certified copy of each death certificate to the lender and closing agent in case they ask for it.

It is important to ascertain whether or not an unnamed person is still living in the home or paying any funds toward the home or the loan balance, and be aware of every name on the note, mortgage, and/or deed. If the home was declared a 'homestead' (the primary residence) in Florida, whoever was married to the primary borrower may need to sign the listing agreement and purchase contract in order to process the short sale, whether or not they are married or live there.

Under certain circumstances the need to handle some of these details can be eliminated if a divorce court divested one of the parties from ownership and a quitclaim deed was recorded.

Again, I don't just take the word of the homeowner; I do my research. Clients often don't know who has a legal interest in what happens to their own property. For example, in cases of divorce the person who signed the note and mortgage may think they are relieved because of a mediated marital agreement or the final divorce decree, but that may not have any effect on the liability or documentation that they initially signed with the lender.

While checking to see who or what is attached to a property might seem easy enough, I have seen a variety of issues arise out of this simple task. In one incident, while preparing for closing the closing agent discovered issues with the title. The title company that had held the previous closing was out of business. This ordeal took several weeks to clear up which delayed the closing and in the process the buyer decided to move on.

Some other situations I have come across are name changes, ownership by a corporation that no longer exists, and even hidden identities.

Name Changes Can Change Everything

In the aftermath of a divorce, a signer on the note and/or mortgage may have had a name change. There have been times when a client uses a middle name as part of their legal name, but that fact is not reflected on the mortgage documents. In those instances the client must get a notarized affidavit showing both versions of the name belong to the same person. In cases of a divorce I ask the client to get me a copy of the final divorce decree and the mediated marital agreement, if any. Copies are sent ahead of the closing date to the lender as well as to the closing agent.

Owned by a Corporate Ghost

The property may have been purchased under a corporation that no longer exists. In a case like this, I brought the situation to the attention of the seller's lawyer who drafted documentation for the last board of directors to become trustees of the corporate assets. I got the lender's negotiator to approve the change. The trustees signed all the documents throughout the process and the closing. We were able to complete the transaction.

Hidden Identities

In some rare cases, usually with politicians, protected witnesses, or undercover law enforcement, the name on the deed may be a pseudonym to protect the identity of the homeowner. I had a client who was a police officer and complying with county law, he had put the name of his ten-year-old daughter as the owner of record in the county clerk's office. From what he told me, this was to protect the entire family from potential reprisals as deeds are in the public record, and criminals could simply go on the Internet and search county records to find the address of their arresting officer. While this makes perfect sense as a way to protect law enforcement officers from criminals' revenge, this can make selling a house difficult when it is time to verify that the signer is in fact the owner, and has the authority to convey the property to the buyer. In the case of my client, we sent the bank a copy of the law allowing for his actions, and we even had all parties sign an affidavit to verify my client's ownership of the property, but to little avail. In the end papers had to be filed with the county to change the name of record on the deed. This was handled by the attorneys and the transaction closed, even though this little diversion delayed the closing by a whole month!

All of these scenarios must be researched and resolved before we can get to the settlement table, otherwise there may not be time to remedy these defects in the title before the foreclosure sale date.

Where Did That Lien Come From?

Before I put a home up for sale, I look for other liens on the property—credit card judgments, IRS liens, mechanics' liens, among others. Any of these could stall a short sale settlement if not handled early. Open permits can also become a problem, so make sure they are all closed.

Also, if there is a homeowners association, be sure it is aware of what is happening and that it is on board with the short sale. Homeowners associations can foreclose faster than a bank in Florida, so you want to check in your state. I had one incident where I lined up a short sale, and somewhere in the middle of the process the homeowners had stopped paying their association dues and they failed to tell their attorney and me. I could not complete the sale and the attorney was helpless as we found out that the homeowners association foreclosed and took title to the property that same day, thereby dispossessing my clients of their interest.

Any of these complications can be avoided if dealt with at the right time and with enough time because it takes time to contact all interested parties. If you are the seller and suspect any of these issues may arise, alert your realtor right away. It is unwise to pretend these problems aren't there or put off facing them. These issues always come to light before closing and if they aren't resolved, it can defeat the whole short sale transaction. Again, that is why I make every effort to address as many issues as I can up-front and handle them early while there is still time.

Is Buyer's Commitment Real or a Waste of Your Time?

The seller's agent must make it clear to all potential buyers that the best way an offer on any short sale property will be taken seriously is if the buyer commits to a reasonable escrow deposit and a pre-qualification letter or proof of funds. If I suspect the property has issues such as black mold, toxic dry wall from China, problems with plumbing, or other environmental hazards, I insist upon a quick inspection. When we get an early inspection it commits the buyer to make a decision to stay in the transaction until the settlement or cancel at that point. It also provides leverage while negotiating with the lender. The inspection report must be from a licensed inspector. I then share that report with the lender who validates the issues with the property and becomes agreeable to the buyer offering a reduced sale price.

I insist on a reasonable deposit, pre-qualification letter, or proof of funds because in a short sale we do not have time to bet on buyers who submit an insincere offer. Once we accept an offer, the seller must remove the property from the market. If the short sale is not approved while the lender is pursuing foreclosure and a judge happens to order a sale date during the processing period, we might not get another offer in time to bring the short sale to settlement.

In transactions over $1 million, an escrow of two to three percent shows the lender or servicing company that the buyer is serious. In smaller short sale transactions, I require the buyer put down at least $5,000 to $10,000 to show they are serious. It's too easy to walk away from a transaction when a buyer has only $1,000 in escrow. In my professional opinion, we must present a solid value proposition to the person negotiating on behalf of the lender for the transaction to gain approval. Finally, the seller's agent needs to be sure the buyer understands that short sales have a longer sales cycle. Completing a short sale usually takes three to five months, sometimes longer. The buyer should not expect a sixty-day closing and then get frustrated.

In transactions where the entire short sale process, including the settlement, must take place within thirty days because of a servicer's transfer or because the property will go to a foreclosure sale, I only accept cash offers. I have closed under these scenarios, but it takes a serious commitment and coordination with all parties involved.

The Value of Empathy

Buyers should keep in mind that most homeowners facing fore-closure are highly emotional due to the difficult circumstances surrounding them. Many want to sell their home to someone who will cherish and value the home as much as they did. I often receive more than one offer with the same monetary value for my short sale listings. Almost always, the buyer who treats the home-owner with respect and shows compassion gets the property. I particularly recall one luxury estate that I sold as a short sale. It needed extensive repairs and renovations, but the buyers saw the full potential of the property. The seller sensed this and it helped us move the transaction forward. As in many of my short sale list-ings, the buyer's caring attitude was crucial to the homeowners choosing to accept their offer. Some buyers seeking to purchase a luxury short sale miss this key element even though they have the financial means. I can't emphasize enough the importance of human understanding and compassion and the effect these have on the seller who typically chooses a buyer who truly loves their home and displays genuine empathy for their situation.

Conclusion

I find that taking these methodical and charismatic approaches allow for all interested parties to be on board. When everyone is aligned, including the lender, agents, sellers, and the buyers, the challenges are diminished, thereby allowing the focus to be on the end goal—getting to the settlement.

Selling or purchasing a home can bring out the best or the worst in people, and short sales are no exception. In my experi-ence the only way to complete the process successfully with mini-mal drama is when agents, sellers, and buyers agree to the ground rules. In that process the listing agent assumes the leadership role and therefore, expertise is essential.

"I always tried to turn every disaster into an opportunity."

—John D. Rockefeller

7

Are Short Sales a Thing of the Past?

Most people associate short sales with the subprime mortgage crisis that the United States experienced right after the housing bubble in mid-2007. But in reality, short sales are an interesting phenomenon that occurs even during a balanced market.

I remember living in Massachusetts in 1990 when I sold my home and I was left with less than a couple thousand dollars. At least my family did not have to bring money to closing, but some of my friends left Massachusetts having to pay more than $40,000 at closing just to sell their home. I also remember in the early to mid-1990s a good number of homeowners in Sacramento, California, were experiencing foreclosures when their defense contract jobs ended.

Back in those days, I recall "upside-down mortgage" was the term used and lenders were reluctant to negotiate with distressed sellers. It seemed that homeowners only had two alternatives: make good on their financial obligations or face foreclosure. Since the housing bubble of 2007 things have changed.

A Listing By Any Other Name Is Still a Listing

For the most part when I list any property, including short sales, I don't treat them any differently than a resale of a luxury home.

I go through the process of staging, taking professional photos, and listing it in all the appropriate places. However, in the case of a short sale there is one difference—I indicate on Multiple Listing System (the MLS) that the property is being sold as a short sale. This difference is important because in any short sale everything hinges upon getting the seller's mortgage lender to approve the sale. This sets a reasonable expectation as any buyer will know they should anticipate a longer cycle to close.

For Sale Signs in Short Sales?

It's important for all parties involved to be sensitive to the fact that listing one's home as a short sale is usually a painful and embarrassing experience for the seller. On several occasions clients were bewildered by the fact that they found themselves in a position where they had to sell their home as a short sale and struggle with the ramifications. This is still a reality for some homeowners today.

For example, I had a client who worked in the financial services industry. In addition to the personal embarrassment, the client wondered how I would be able to market and sell the property without impacting his career. I assured the client that we would be able to do this discreetly. We would forget the "For Sale" sign in front of the house but go ahead and list it as a short sale on the MLS. That seemed to satisfy my client.

As the listing agent I regard the homeowner with genuine empathy and understanding. The circumstances that lead up to a short sale often come by way of forces outside of the homeowner's control. Some have faced a rapid decline in income, going from a high six or seven-figure salary to a survival wage that fails to meet their debt service, and while this description is relative, it is nonetheless real to each unique family. Others have had unfortunate circumstances like a divorce, death of a loved one, or an illness. Any of these shifts can deflate even the most resilient of people. That is why I believe it is important to have empathy and understanding for the people who reach out for my help. Having gone through a short sale myself, I know the spectrum of emotions that are endured. But I survived and found a way to move forward. I share my confidence with my clients.

Once I feel they are receptive, I explain the process prior to listing their home and the reasons I believe my recommendations would work best to achieve the desired outcome. Listing a short sale alongside traditional resale properties gives us an advantage. In a traditional resale the seller often thinks the property is worth more than fair market value. Therefore, the listing agent has to placate the homeowner and start with a higher price than they know they can achieve. However, in a short sale, due to the sense of urgency to sell the home before it forecloses, we establish a realistic price early on so the home stands out as a great value among higher priced properties.

Pricing Strategies

In the distressed luxury market, I have two winning strategies that I use frequently. One is pricing the home below market value and the other is pricing slightly over market value.

There are a couple of situations where starting out pricing the home below the market is best. If the house is in a hot market and in excellent condition, I list it at about seven to ten percent under market value. This may seem counter intuitive. You may ask, "Why not price it at the top if it's a great home in a great market?" I find that when we price the home on the lower side in seller's markets it attracts more interest. People flock to the property and that kicks off a bidding war. When I use this strategy I often end up selling the home at a price above its current market value.

In 2012 I worked with a homeowner who felt I had priced the property too low. Other agents without extensive short sale experience told my client that they could get five to seven percent higher than the price I had suggested. I told my client, "Trust me, my strategy will give you the best chance to avoid foreclosure and a deficiency judgment." My client trusted me and agreed to proceed. I am always aware of my win-win-win philosophy. I proceeded to price the house at seven percent below the fair market value. The first day we created such frenzy that people were standing in line outside the house waiting for their turn. We had offers galore. Buyers were outbidding each other left and right. By the time we concluded the showings, the selling price was twelve percent higher than the asking price. The bank was so pleased they accepted the offer right away. Even though this was a challenging short sale, we were able to close within three short months. I recognize that other agents' approaches differ from mine and I respect that, but just like in other fields, experts don't always agree.

In another example I was dealing with an obstinate tenant who would only allow showings one day per week during a four-hour window. Nevertheless, I signed on for the challenge because I knew this property was in A-quality condition in an A-quality location. Remember, it's about making lemonade from lemons. In the description of the short sale listing I provided imagery to get potential buyers thinking of the lifestyle they could have if they bought the home. Again, realtors and their clients lined up waiting their turn to see the property. Some people had to park several blocks away due to the multitude of interested buyers. Then the bidding war started. I had realtors calling me making offers and saying, "If you get a higher offer, let me know before you accept it."

I kept telling them, "Give me your best and highest now because I can't be calling people back. And my client would prefer a cash offer."

One realtor responded on the spot by making a cash offer for nineteen percent above the asking price on behalf of her client, and her client won the bidding war. Because it was a cash offer, I knew it would close without any complications that may arise when dealing with a buyer's financing. The end result was a successful closing and a release of the deficiency.

Marketing Still a Must

Distressed homeowners must remember that succumbing to a financial crisis situation doesn't define who they are. Still, it's a bag full of mixed emotions including shame, disappointment, and failure. I understand the importance of privacy for most of my clients. So I sit down with the homeowner and go over my marketing checklist. I show them all the options available for marketing the property and allow the homeowner to give input on which methods they find agreeable.

Most homeowners' number one objection is placing a sign in front of their property. I understand distressed homeowners' psyches; they don't want to broadcast the news to the neighborhood. Being a techie at my core, I have only placed one sign on the ground since the inception of my career. Give me the Internet any day! But if the homeowner allows it, I do go up and down the block and knock on neighbors' doors to see if they know anyone who is in the market for a home in the area.

It is Not Personal

Once a buyer decides to extend an offer to purchase a property, the process of selling a home as a short sale significantly differs from a traditional resale and each special condition must be met in order to close. Regardless of how you negotiate or with whom, the short sale transaction must be set up in a way that all parties involved get a win. For this to happen, it is imperative to understand who the parties are and be clear on what is at stake for each. When you understand the various parties' needs and wants you will be empowered to create the best-case scenario for everyone. There is always the possibility to create a win-win-win as long as everyone has reasonable expectations.

It Comes Down to the Agent

The seller's agent must assume the leadership role and use his or her best efforts to establish a solid professional relationship with the buyer's agent. Additionally, I find that if the agent representing the buyer has limited experience in the short sale process, I take the time to educate them. In my experience this provides the seller's agent an opportunity to assess the likelihood of completing the settlement. The worst thing that can happen is when a homeowner removes the house from the market for months, only to have the buyer run off chasing some newly listed foreclosure. Often, in situations where the potential buyer fails to follow through, the homeowner doesn't have enough time left to find another buyer before facing their own foreclosure sale date. Because there are fewer potential buyers in the luxury market, I don't just take the word of the buyer's agent that their buyer is solid. I always do my best to meet the buyer face-to-face and make my own evaluation. Buyer credibility improves greatly with a responsible deposit, prequalification letter, or proof of funds.

It's in the buyer's agent's best interest to not only protect the buyer's best interests but to help move the process along. Knowledgeable agents who stay up-to-date on new short sale listings as they enter the market can present their clients with exceptional opportunities to acquire property at highly competitive prices. But not all buyers' agents know how to manage a short sale. Anyone thinking of purchasing a short sale property should interview their realtor to make sure that the agent understands how to structure a short sale offer and has worked through several successful short sale transactions. The chances of success greatly increase when selecting an agent with the pedigree, knowledge, and a confirmed, superior track record.

Time to Go to the Lender

Once the seller accepts an offer, the seller's realtor or whoever is handling the processing of the sale must submit the short sale package to the seller's lender. This is where I believe the entire team needs to be engaged. Lenders require financial information such as tax returns, bank statements, etc. A realtor can only be a conduit and pass these documents on to the lender. More often than not, this is when a sophisticated client may ask about asset protection, estate planning issues, and responsibility for any deficiency they may face. Only a lawyer can provide all these answers. Know your strengths and know your limitations. Ride your strengths and shore up your limitations by engaging the right experts.

Next, the lender approves, counters, or rejects the offer, depending on the net loss the investor will accept. This is the make or break moment for the only way the sale can happen is with the lender's approval. We must get the lender to agree to accept less than the original repayment amount and release the lien on the property. Unfortunately, unless the short sale is pre-approved, the person negotiating with the bank isn't made privy to the magic number that will get the short sale approved. This is where performing early inspections and understanding the market makes a difference. For example, I sold one property where the bank wanted $2 million to release the lien. We were able to procure an offer of $1.3 million. At first the bank wanted to reject the offer but we were able to show through an early inspection that the property had a raccoon infestation, termites, and black mold. The bank lowered their expectations and approved the sale.

I sometimes see realtors who open with an emotional plea and take the homeowner's personal plight to the bank. This ineffective strategy wastes precious time. While any communication with the lender or servicer has become less stressful over the years, make no mistake, this is about a business mitigating the loss of the investor holding the note. We need to approach the bank with an acceptable business proposition, and that has nothing to do with the situation of why the homeowner can't pay, how hard they've tried, or what they've been through. Two distinct "show me" criteria always ring clear from the lender's perspective, and these are:

1. Make it commercially reasonable.

2. Show me the MONEY.

Any time that I need to negotiate with the lender to lower the desired price the best approach I have found is to mentally step into the shoes of the investor. Just like with any presentation, we need to know the audience, and in this case that audience is the lender. So the first thing I think of is, "What do they need to know?"

Since the investor wants to mitigate the loss, I have to provide credible data to justify why the investor must take a greater loss. By taking this approach, I realized early on that my documentation must be solid.

In one case my clients were forced to sell their property due to a divorce. After living in their home for sixteen years they needed to short sale the property. Their residence was in a beautiful location near a nature preserve with wooded surroundings. It had been well cared for, but unbeknownst to them, a local company had been dumping toxic waste into nearby streams and had contaminated the drinking water. There were also more than one thousand cases of cancer reported near the area, many of which were found in children. In researching further I found that the Florida Department of Health had declared the area a "Pediatric Cancer Cluster."

In Florida a real estate agent must disclose any matters adversely affecting the value of the property. Often, the lender doesn't know the local market. For that reason it was my responsibility to disclose these matters, which I knew would have an impact on the pricing of the home. It was evident that I had to educate the lender with factual information from the Florida Department of Health. This information also included recent statistics on area home sales, which had fallen drastically to seventy percent of prior market value.

I could have gone to the lender with a sob story about their broken marriage or all the sick kids in the area. But what made the difference was that I supplied factual data which proved why the lender would never procure the price they had assigned to the property. My letter and the supporting data convinced the lender to cut their losses, approve the short sale, and relieve my clients of the deficiency.

Negotiations with the lender can become even more complex when other entities get involved. For example, I had a short sale in which the lender was using an auction company to validate pricing on all offers received. The auction house validates pricing by including the property on their website to see how many offers they solicit. If the listing price is too low, generally a slew of offers will be posted on their website within a short time frame.

I had an offer of $718,000 that I presented to the lender, which was close to the top of the fair market value of $725,000. The auction company then put the property up on their website for sale at $718,000. For those who visited the auction company's website they could not clearly see that the sale price did not include the auction company's fees. After these additional fees the actual sale price would have totaled around $750,000, an amount way above the market price and impossible to sell. The auction company had it on the website for a month with no offers. Meanwhile, the buyer that I had procured became frustrated and walked away.

Then the auction company went ahead and arbitrarily reduced the asking price by $200,000. Yes, that is correct—$200,000 less. When I saw that change I immediately contacted the lender. With a potential high loss to the lender I was concerned that if the sale went through, the lender would insist that my client be responsible for all or part of the deficiency. I explained to the negotiator each of the wrong assumptions the auction company had made and then proceeded to ask for a chance to find another buyer to match the original purchase contract. I knew we could get $718,000 for that house, but my concern was that once I procured a new contract I would be right back where I started with the auction company doing their "validation process" again. So I negotiated with the lender that once I found a new buyer, the short sale would be processed directly with the lender and not through the auction company. The lender agreed to provide me the opportunity to procure an offer close to $718,000 but only gave me one week to find a buyer. Sometimes the real estate angels are on our side, and within that week we received a new offer for $718,000.

I presented the fully executed contract to the lender, but it turned out no one in the lender's office had informed the auction company. The auction company, unbeknownst to everyone, had received a bid that was $202,000 less than the contract I sent the lender. I worked closely with the seller's attorney and we both approached the lender. The seller's attorney had his client sign the $718,000 contract immediately. Then the attorney communicated to the lender and the auction company that his client had signed a $718,000 offer. The attorney went on to explain that signing more than one contract would have placed the homeowner in a legally compromising position. At the same time I presented the issue to the lender's CEO. I am not saying that I call financial institutions' CEOs for every short sale, but in this transaction I found it necessary to get his attention. I left the CEO a message advocating on behalf of their stockholders. It went something like this, "All financial institutions have a business practice of doing what is in the best interest of their shareholders and losing $200,000 is not in the best interest of anyone but the auction company. Imagine if twenty such transactions went through where each netted a loss of $200,000. That would be a hefty amount to lose. You probably agree with me that $4,000,000 is a good chunk of money by any standard."

That message initiated interest and subsequent action from the lender. In the end the seller's attorney was able to get the attention of a vice president at the lending institution; within three months the short sale closed and the seller was released from the deficiency.

Make a Paper Trail

In some markets there is a higher occurrence of foreclosure fraud and South Florida is one of those markets, so I am extra careful with documentation. I document every conversation I have with lenders, clients, and other agents. I recommend that any agent dealing with short sales do the same. Fraud can happen anywhere, and if you accidentally get caught up in it you will be glad you have documentation to prove that you acted properly.

> There is a lot to be learned in dealing with short sales and meticulous documentation is one of the most crucial practices in any real estate transaction.

In one short sale we were close to receiving the approval. At the last minute and for no apparent reason, the negotiator for the bank wanted to switch to a new title company. According to the negotiator, the bank had selected a new title company to complete the short sale. I saw a red flag. I sent an email thanking the negotiator for the conversation, reiterating the details of the discussion and what I had been instructed to do.

On the day I was supposed to get the approval letter, I received a call from the negotiator, but it was from a non-bank number. Later that day I received two other voice messages: one call was from a vice president of the bank and it clearly had originated from a bank number and the other call was from the new negotiator assigned to the file. I decided to wait and listen to all the voice messages before responding to anyone. It turns out the bank terminated the negotiator that I had been working with due to the negotiator engaging in side deals without the bank's approval or authority, and our transaction was one of several that had come under scrutiny. I proactively shared with the vice president all the information and the documentation of every conversation between the former negotiator and me. After the bank had audited the file, I was advised that my documentation clearly showed that I had not been part of any wrongdoing. A week later the lender issued an approval and we proceeded to settlement.

Playing Games with the Lender Gets You Nowhere

On another short sale I was working with a homeowner as the listing agent of a luxury estate. I also represented the buyer, but while I was waiting to get the signed offer back, the seller contacted me saying, "Norka, I would like you to get me an extension of six months after the buyer purchases my home since many of my friends have received extensions."

To that I responded, "I can't do that. Your lender would not allow it and even if the lender allowed that kind of arrangement, I can't see any reason for the buyer to agree to make mortgage payments for six months without taking possession of their property while you live in it. Besides, there is an arm's length transaction affidavit that would prohibit that type of arrangement." I knew the lender would not accept that arrangement because I had dealt with that lender many times before. My client, the homeowner, kept saying, "but my friends have done it. Everyone I know has."

I explained that I was not going to sign an arm's length transaction affidavit knowing the seller was not relinquishing possession at settlement. Finally, I indicated that neither the buyer nor I would get involved in such a transaction. My client then accused me of trying to cheat them and called me worthless. Since my answer provoked the seller's indignation, I requested a termination of the listing and documented the facts surrounding the termination. At a later date, I received a call from the lender and I explained why I was no longer the realtor involved in that short sale. That was the last I heard from the lender.

I soon found out that my former client eventually found a realtor who was willing to work in the seller's creative ways. I can only assume that when the lender found out what the seller was trying to do, the lender was not willing to play along because in the end, the lender foreclosed on the property.

Community Associations—Friend or Foe?

Negotiations with condo or homeowners associations while processing a short sale sometimes leave me wondering "Why was this so difficult?"

In the luxury market the contractual relationship between the homeowner and the community association often goes much deeper than just dues. Homeowners may pay equity membership deposits of $60,000 to $90,000 or more. When there is a need to make a short sale, the association can impose a lien on these funds against delinquent dues.

Frequently, a homeowner struggling to pay a mortgage also stops paying the community association dues, whether it is a condo or homeowners association (HOA). Most homeowners do not realize that the condo or HOA has the right to foreclose when the homeowner's payments become delinquent. In Florida a community association's foreclosure can move to a judicial sale faster than a lender's foreclosure proceeding.

I have seen community associations foreclose and take possession of a property, then rent it to a third party until the lender completes its foreclosure. So if your property is located in a community regulated by an association, and you are struggling to pay the dues, try to work out some payment plan. Some of my clients have been able to negotiate a forbearance plan with the association while getting them to hold off on pursuing a foreclosure. Unfortunately, it's never guaranteed.

At times when the homeowner has failed to keep current with the dues, the arrears accumulate to a substantial amount. In those instances I ask the homeowner to obtain a current statement from the association so I can facilitate the negotiations between the lender and the association.

You may ask why is this so critical? If the homeowner is not in good standing, the association will most likely not issue an approval to the prospective buyer and the short sale will fail. In some cases I have to ask the buyer to contribute the difference, which can become another sticking point in closing the short sale settlement.

This is where the power of negotiation can come in handy. I am reminded of one case where the homeowner became delinquent by $24,000 in HOA dues, late fees, and legal fees. I was able to negotiate a reduction to $13,000, and we completed the short sale.

Often when I am speaking with bank's negotiators, they comment about how powerful the associations are in Florida. Even when the dues are current, the condo or HOA has the right to forestall the settlement by delaying the potential buyer's approval, delaying the estoppel letter, and causing various other problems. Condos or HOA documents vary from community to community, so it's important to make sure the seller's attorney and buyer's attorney review these documents. I make it a practice to review them to determine if there are any restrictions such as no pets or a limit of one assigned parking space or storage unit.

Right of First Refusal: The Bane of Short Sales

It's not lady-like to swear, but when a community association exercises their right of first refusal, I am truly tempted! Let me explain. Let's say the lender approves the short sale at $1 million. If documents provide for the association to have the right of first refusal, the association has the right to step in and substitute itself as the buyer under the exact same terms of the initial buyer's contract. This move eliminates the initial buyer and any other pending transaction.

What makes it difficult and arouses my desire to curse is that once the association exercises their right of first refusal, the lender requires us to go through the entire process before we get approved to substitute the association as the buyer. If the last Broker's Price Opinion (BPO) is older than sixty to ninety days, the lender will request an update. If the new BPO comes back with a higher sale price, the association may reject the increase and terminate the contract. At that point the agent must either go back to the initial buyer, hat in hand, and try to get them back on board at the higher price or look for a new buyer, despite having spent all that time and energy with the original buyer.

And to give it a dash of "I hate you," the association can step in again and substitute into the transaction of the new buyer. A seller is almost guaranteed to hate the realtor and anyone else associated with the transaction, especially the association for trapping them on a merry-go-round. Real estate is a people business, and some agents will take any action by the association as a sign that the seller should have known better and that you are wasting their time—regardless of how powerless you are, they will remember your name with a voodoo doll attached. Change just one term or condition in a new contract and the HOA gets a new right of refusal.

My advice is to get all association governing documents as early in the process as possible and review them. It will help you to be prepared and decide ahead of time the best strategy.

Know the Community

Before listing or making an offer on a home that's part of an association, be sure you know the composition of owners versus tenants in the complex. Lenders believe a condo complex occupied primarily by homeowners is less risky than one with a lot of rental units. Many lenders won't give a buyer a loan if the complex has too high of a ratio of tenants to owners. Therefore, it is important to know these statistics so when the property is marketed all this is taken into consideration when developing a strategy.

In short sale transactions the seller must convey a clear title, so in many cases the seller's lender will need to give up a portion of the short sale proceeds for the association to release its lien. Usually the amount the lender offers is Florida statutory driven and less than the total debt the homeowner owes. A problem can arise when the HOA wants the debt paid in full and the lender doesn't want to offer more than a specified amount of the sale proceeds. If the HOA refuses to accept the amount offered by the seller's lender and other arrangements are not made, the short sale will fail to close.

Because condo and homeowners associations are usually non-profit organizations, they need an operating budget that covers their operating expenses. A well-managed association will have adequate reserves for repairs and replacements of the common areas and any other elements of the properties the association maintains. In communities where a substantial number of homeowners have past due balances, new buyers who want to purchase and require financing may be rejected due to the poor state of the association's finances. It often happens that the association's budget is not adequate to repair and maintain common areas that fall into disrepair. This detracts from the community's appearance and perceived value, and the potential buyer's lender may be unwilling to provide financing for properties in such a community. Savvy buyers and agents check the financial health of the association and make that issue a contingency in their offer.

Bottom line, in a short sale the property transfer can only occur with a clear title and this can only be accomplished when the association releases their lien and approves the buyer.

One Step Closer

The best part of being a luxury short sales expert aside from seeing the relieved faces of my clients when they no longer have the 600-pound gorilla of the bank's demands weighing on them, is when the lender sends their letter approving the short sale. It usually comes out of the blue and without any pre-announcement. You receive an email or fax of the lender's approval after what feels like skating uphill for the previous few months. When the investor that owns the loan approves the loss for the sale of the property and agrees to proceed to settlement, you know the hardest part has passed. After you take a deep breath, a sigh of relief may overtake you as you sit down and begin slowly reading the approval letter. I feel this way after every approval letter because I know I have helped someone move forward to a new life, even if it's just a little step.

Still, an approval letter does not, by any means, indicate that everything is "good to go." In fact, there are still lots of things that can go wrong. People often don't understand that an approval letter means nothing if the short sale does not close.

The approval letter usually lists numerous terms and conditions upon which the short sale is contingent. The items to look for in the approval letter include:

- Minimum net proceeds the lender will accept from the sale transaction. Make sure the net proceeds match on the HUD-1 to be approved prior to closing by the seller's lender and on the closing disclosure.

- Closing date—the last date for the short sale to close and for the seller's lender to receive the funds via wire transfer. In most cases the closing date can be extended as long as no judicial sale date has been set and the lender provides a new approval letter.

- Commissions and the amount the lender is willing to pay the realtors at closing. Commissions reduce the net proceeds of the sale so the lender must approve the amounts.

- Acceptable Settlement Charges—these charges must be displayed on the HUD-1 to be approved prior to closing by the seller's lender and on the closing disclosure.

- Payoff to Subordinate Liens—this is the payoff amount allowed by the first mortgage lien holder to subordinate junior liens. The junior liens could be second or third mortgages or lines of credit, real estate tax liens, mechanics' liens, homeowners association liens, etc.

- Arm's Length Transaction affidavits to be notarized at closing. Most approval letters have a stipulation that requires all parties engaged in the transaction represent that they are not engaged in any transactions outside of closing without the lender's knowledge and approval. Beware, as a violation of this affidavit carries with it federal criminal penalties.

- Closing and wiring instructions—these details are for the closing agent on how the funds are to be transferred to the lender with a date and time they are to be received.

- Promissory note—the lender has the right to insist that the homeowner be responsible for a certain amount of the loss on the short sale, and those terms will be included in the approval letter.

After reviewing the approval letter, I immediately send a copy to the closing agent, seller's attorney, buyer's attorney, and buyer's agent. Since I work closely with a team of attorneys on all of my short sales, the seller's attorney goes over the details of the terms with the seller and answers any questions the clients may have. If there is any promissory note attached the attorney reviews that as well.

While waiting for the approval letter everyone should be busy getting the other final pieces in place. I have seen clients get an approval letter and still be unable to close for a number of reasons. Let's look at some of the most common issues that can cause a settlement to fail after the lender approves the sale.

Financing Issues

Some buyers have such a strong credit score that even when they are financing the purchase of the property on a short sale, they do not make the contract contingent on their ability to get financing. But that is the exception, not the rule. As people recover from the great recession more buyers need to obtain financing, and a few things can undermine or stop the transaction. Some of the most common problems are: buyers fail to qualify, interest rates fluctuate, and more. In this section we will go into more detail.

Buyer Fails to Qualify

As solid as a buyer may appear when signing the contract, a lot of things can happen to prevent a buyer from qualifying for the purchase. There could be any number of reasons why buyers don't qualify—a change in employment or life circumstances, a change in interest rates, strict requirements from their lender, missed deadlines, or delays. Irrespective of the reasons, if a buyer fails to qualify it adversely impacts the seller's short sale.

Some lenders allow five business days to replace the buyer under the same terms as the initial contract. This is great because the new buyer does not have to wait weeks for the whole short sale process.

Unfortunately, many institutions do not allow the original buyer's contract to be replaced with a successor. In those circumstances the seller and new buyer have to start at least some of the process over to obtain a short sale approval. Other financial institutions require the short sale process to start from scratch.

Interest Rate Fluctuation

The majority of lenders will not give a buyer a lock on a loan interest rate until the short sale is approved, which can take anywhere from eight to twelve weeks or more. The interest rate lock usually expires after thirty or sixty days, and the buyer may have to pay a fee to keep the original quoted rate. If the interest rates happen to swing upward, the buyer may find that the increase in payment affects their ability to qualify for the loan due to the debt-to-income ratio.

Buyer's Loan Processing—Are We There Yet?

Most negotiators want to close a short sale within thirty days of approval. Some loans such as a VA, FHA, and Jumbo VA have a longer approval process. In those cases the closing will take longer than thirty days. Be sure to make any lien holder aware that the buyer is going through a loan approval process that will take longer than conventional loans and request a longer period for the buyer to complete their financing. Otherwise you will have to go back and request an extension. There are no guarantees that an extension will be approved.

Buyer's Lender Requires Repairs

Conventional mortgage lenders require the property to appraise for a certain amount and are less involved with the details of the property. Those lenders have minimum requirements for a property's condition to write a loan. On the other hand, loans like FHA, upon reviewing the appraisal and inspection report, may request fixing some of the repairs needed. I recall that in one of my short sales the VA requested the replacement of the outside AC unit which had been stolen. The seller generally does not have the resources to make substantial repairs, and even if they did, the seller's lien holder may insist the money that the seller would have spent on repairs be paid to the seller's lender instead.

Short sale lenders will rarely pay for repairs. Most short sales are sold in "as is" condition. But some negotiators may lower the sale price if adverse findings stipulate a problem that poses a hazard—yet another reason to have the inspection done early.

Inspection Issues

When inspections are done after the approval letter arrives, unforeseen issues can discourage the buyer or require the seller to go back to the seller's lender to re-negotiate the sale price. In one of my short sales the inspection was done after the approval. It revealed that the property had a bad breaker panel that was a fire hazard. When the buyer's lender had the home appraised the value came back considerably lower than the contract price. I had to renegotiate with the seller's lender to get the contract price to match the appraisal or the short sale would not have closed. I was successful in negotiating a partial reduction, but the buyer had to add personal funds to make up the difference of their own lender's appraisal.

Back in 2009 at the beginning of my real estate career, I had a transaction where the short sale fell apart because the buyer canceled the contract after reading the results of the inspection report. The short sale process went on for months before we received the approval letter, and only then did the buyer order the inspection. Once he obtained the results of the inspection he requested a price reduction of $80,000, but the lender did not agree. I had to look for a subsequent buyer and restart the short sale process. That lesson made me aware of how important it is for buyers to order an inspection within days of the purchase contract being executed by all parties. In my experience I find that it's best to start any negotiations with the seller's lender with as much information as possible, and having an inspection report helps everyone understand the condition of the property. I strongly recommend using the inspection report as part of the negotiation package. Since time wasted is enemy #1 in short sales, if the transaction is going to fail due to a bad inspection, the sooner everyone knows the better.

In the end, since short sales and foreclosures have been and always will be the consequence of a downturn in the economy, there will always be a need to understand this segment of the real estate market. As I demonstrated in chapter 5, falling behind on mortgage payments occurs without discrimination of rich or poor.

Other Delays

I have experienced that in the resale of real estate, even traditional sales with conventional or jumbo loans, delays in the buyer's financing process are inevitable. Surveyors and appraisers can be late with reports, underwriting may take longer than usual, or the buyer could be waiting for financial documentation from another country. Regardless of the reason, the best course is to count on delays rather than count on everything going according to plan. One way to avert or shorten delays is to have the buyer's agent call the buyer's lender frequently and sometimes every day to check on the loan's progress. This way the buyer's loan package stays on top of the stack. Also, we become aware right away of any issues that arise, and thus, we have more time to manage them.

Do We Have a Match?—Community Association and Buyer's Approval

It is important to remember that even if the homeowner is current with dues, the HOA can hinder the closing of the short sale transaction in other ways.

- HOA rejecting the buyer. If you are planning to buy a short sale property that is part of an HOA, beware of what you post on social media. HOA and Condo associations, especially in the luxury market, have the right to refuse potential buyers. I know of at least one incident where the buyer's teenage children were posting things on Facebook that the HOA deemed inappropriate. The HOA refused to allow their parents to purchase the home. In another case a client had a DUI arrest on his record. His purchase was also denied. Bottom line, aside from discriminating based on race or gender, the HOA pretty much has the right to deny anyone they want, and they use it and sometimes abuse it. Most buyers prefer not to become embroiled in a court battle and therefore, they move on.

- Buyer rejecting the HOA. If the HOA is low on cash due to too many residents being late on dues or poor management, the buyer may decide to cancel the purchase contract or try to negotiate an even lower price.

- Timing. Most associations have a screening and approval process. If the prospective owner/buyer fails to apply within a reasonable time before closing, the short sale could fail to close. Make sure that as a buyer or buyer's agent you know how much time is needed to process the application. In addition, some associations require meeting a prospective owner in person, so if the buyer travels often or lives part of the time in another country or state make sure to plan accordingly.

"Strategy without tactics is the slowest route to victory. Tactics without strategy is the noise before defeat."

—Sun Tzu

8

Getting to the Finish Line

After the approval the key to completing any short sale is getting the transaction to close on time. Therefore, it is important to remember the seller's lender is the entity that sets the deadline in the approval letter. But the title company/closing agent must understand the short sale process so they can work with all parties involved and manage the inevitable last minute details.

Even though a short sale closing is similar to the closing of a traditional real estate transaction, a few issues unique to short sale can ruin the closing. That is where short sales are tricky. In this chapter I will explain what these issues are and share best practices to prevent them.

Pre-close

Before everyone gets to go to the closing table there are a few more steps to complete. Unfortunately, if there is a judicial sale date already set, the time left to close could be less than thirty days prior to the judicial sale date. Most lenders only allocate up to thirty days to close from the date of the approval letter. In other cases I have seen lenders cancel a scheduled judicial sale to allow a short sale closing to take place. If you are involved in a short sale process and have thirty days to close be sure to initiate pre-closing work within a sufficient time frame to close on schedule.

Buyer's Responsibilities

Once the sale is approved, the buyer's first responsibility is to get the approval letter to the mortgage broker or loan officer, update his or her application, and order the property to be appraised right away. It is vital to be sure the property's appraised value is equal to or greater than the sale price. For example, if the short sale was approved at one price and the buyer's lender's appraisal comes back with an amount that is lower than the approved sale price, the buyer has three options: one is to make up the difference in cash; the second is to ask the seller's agent to renegotiate the sale price with the seller's lender; and the third is to walk away. The first two options can take two weeks or more, so the sooner the buyer's lender appraises the home, the better. If you are the buyer's agent, make sure you are in constant communication with your client's mortgage broker or loan officer so you can provide any documentation needed without delay.

Seller's Responsibilities

An experienced seller's agent will work closely with the closing agent, buyer's lender, and the buyer's agent, and keep the seller informed of progress and/or setbacks. Furthermore, the seller's agent will work with the seller to provide access to the appraiser hired by the buyer's lender. The seller's agent must strongly emphasize to the seller the importance of keeping the agent apprised of any new incidents against the property that might show up on the closing agent's title search.

I had a short sale that I thought was ready to close, but the seller's ex-wife decided to place a lien on the property. The seller's attorney could not get the lien removed quickly enough to close, so the home went to a foreclosure sale.

In another case I had a short sale where we learned at closing that there was an outstanding order from the city set to trigger two days after the closing and impose a lien against the property for a substantial amount of money per day for failure to construct a child-proof barrier fence around a swimming pool. We were able to solve the issue by having the closing agent hold escrow to cover two weeks of daily penalties. In addition, I had to negotiate with the buyers to make an immediate application for a permit to construct the fence and to pay to have it built. We were lucky to close under those circumstances.

Tick Tock

Regardless of the number of days given on the approval letter, time is ticking and in the case of short sales, getting an extension becomes difficult. Therefore, it is important that all parties involved cooperate to complete any reasonable actions that must be taken prior to closing and comply with all closing requirements in an expedient manner.

Neither the buyer's nor the seller's agent should feel that their role begins and ends by merely identifying problems that may hinder the closing of the short sale. If you encounter a problem and have a possible solution in mind, propose it to all parties involved at the same time you present the problem. In the case of title issues, I prefer to present such problems to the seller's attorney or an attorney on my team so we can work through the problem with the right expertise. If the buyer suspects a major problem they may decide not to move forward. Always try to portray all issues in a positive light and keep moving forward toward a solution. In this business success is all about overcoming obstacles to get to settlement.

Unforeseen Liens

Generally the title company checks for any encumbrances and title issues that may prevent them from issuing a clean title within 30 days prior to closing. In my experience it is a good practice to check for liens at the beginning of the short sale process and again right after you get the approval letter just to be sure nothing new arises. Make sure the party will pay for the search since it's not a free service. In the end, however, it is worth the expense.

Just to give you an idea, some liens like credit cards or other unsecured liens take up to forty-five days to resolve in Florida using an administrative process. Therefore, you may need to file for an extension from the seller's lender and again they are not to be taken for granted. One tricky lien to watch out for is a water lien. Water utilities are city or municipal liens. Therefore, any unpaid bill, even a $30 water bill, can result in the water company placing a lien on the property and this needs to be dealt with for the title company to issue a clean title. I have seen water liens as high as $1,000, in which case it becomes a negotiation to see who will accept responsibility. If the seller pays they must bring a receipt to closing. If the buyer pays it must be added to the HUD-1 settlement statement.

Choosing the Right Closing Date

To have a less stressful closing, I always try to schedule the closing a couple of days before the lender's final expiration date. That way if any problems arise there is time to deal with them before the deadline stipulated on the approval letter. Otherwise, the short sale approval could expire and the closing can't take place.

When unforeseen circumstances appear to delay the closing, it is important to request an extension as soon as possible. In circumstances where we can't get an extension and the closing is set for the last day of the approval letter deadline, the closing might need to happen first thing in the morning of the final day to allow the pay-off wire to be sent to the lender so it arrives on the same day.

Avoid Scheduling on Holidays

We live in a multi-cultural society and one person's workday is another person's holiday. Be aware of this when setting a closing date or you may be in for an unhappy surprise.

One great example of this is when I had a short sale in which all the parties involved were Jewish—the seller, the realtors, the closing agent, and the buyer. The closing date the bank had set happened to fall on Yom Kippur, considered by Jews to be one of the "high holy days" during which it is deemed inappropriate to do any business transactions. Since the short sale purchase was financed and the buyer's lender could not move the date earlier I asked for an extension. At first the lender denied it, but once I explained the importance of the holiday and I pointed out that the bank would never have set a closing date on Christmas day, the closing officer granted an extension.

Regardless of who is involved, be sure to check the closing date against the calendar of government holidays. Also check with the buyer, the seller, and the title company to see if the closing date conflicts with any of their private scheduling considerations, including religious holidays.

Choose a Closing Company That Has Short Sale Experience

The title company does more than just sit with the buyer and seller at closing. In a short sale there are special circumstances that can impede the closing if they are not handled properly—namely, the hard deadline of a judicial sale date.

When the closing date is set near the deadline of the home going into a foreclosure sale, the title company needs to make sure that they have completed a lien search and title search early enough to have time to resolve any issues that might show up as an encumbrance against the title. Otherwise, any adverse issues will need to be handled at closing, and that puts the whole short sale transaction at risk.

In a traditional resale transaction either the buyer or seller may choose the closing agent. But with a short sale I always try to insist upon a closing agent with extensive short sales experience. In a short sale the title company gets involved early in the process because they prepare a preliminary HUD-1 for each lender that has a lien against the seller's property. This preliminary HUD-1 contains all the financial information the seller's lender uses to identify the expenses related to the closing and the net amount going back to them. For example, if there is a first and second mortgage on the home, the title company needs to create a HUD-1 for each lender.

As I strongly suggested earlier, the title company handling the closing of the short sale must order the title commitment early in the process. In one case the title company didn't have enough experience with short sales and they thought they could just use the title commitment that the buyer's agent had received from the buyer's lender. But that is not an approved process in a short sale. This error could have resulted in a failed transaction. Luckily, I was able negotiate and move the closing to the buyer's lawyer who happened to own a title company. We closed on time.

"Make or Break" Details

Short sale closings typically have more details and specific instructions than your traditional real estate closings. To start, the lender's approval letter contains a variety of instructions everyone must implicitly follow in order to close. Not adhering to the conditions in the approval letter jeopardizes the sale.

A typical short sale approval letter includes the closing instructions, the net amount due to the sellers' lenders, and the date all funds must be wired to them. All parties should closely check the preliminary closing disclosure against what the seller's lender expects to net as detailed in the approval letter.

Often the seller's lender specifies they want to receive the final HUD-1 for them to review forty-eight hours prior to closing. The person negotiating directly with the seller's lender sends the HUD-1 at the time specified or the lender may send it back and not issue a final approval to close on time. Also, if the closing agent makes mistakes on the HUD-1 the lender may hold up the sale until they're corrected.

The most demanding closing conditions I ever faced were in a short sale where the lender approved the short sale and provided only ten days to close. The tight deadline complicated matters because the buyer had to get approval from the condominium association. Fortunately, this was a cash transaction and we were able to close within that compressed time. We barely made it and the stress level was through the roof.

Documentation Is (Still) Everything

As I indicated in earlier chapters, it is important to document all communications when moving through the short sale process up to and through the closing. This includes documenting communication with my clients, seller's lender, buyer's agent, and any other party involved.

I once had two clients, a husband and wife, who were hoping to get their relocation expenses covered. The wife procrastinated turning in the required documents to the negotiator. I sent several emails reminding her of the importance of sending in her documents on time and I kept all of those emails. When the negotiator didn't receive the requested documentation on time, he just moved the file along and did not allocate anything for relocation. At closing there were no funds on the HUD-1 settlement statement for relocation expenses. When the husband saw this he complained and refused to sign. It had occurred to me that he might not be aware of his wife's failure to provide the documentation. I came prepared for this possibility and brought the entire correspondence history to show why the relocation funds were not provided. Once he saw the error had been on his side of the table, he signed and we closed without them receiving any relocation expenses. It is sad when homeowners have to leave without anything in their pocket, but they say 90% of success is showing up, and in this case the sellers didn't show up until the last moment.

Beware of Short Sale Fraud

Short sale fraud is a serious problem that is on the rise. As of 2015, Florida has been the leader in this category for several years, according to the LexisNexis Mortgage Fraud report.

The penalties are extremely steep and may include up to thirty years in prison and/or a fine up to one million dollars or more! A short sale fraud conviction can also result in the loss of professional licenses and lawsuits for civil damages. Short sale fraud seems to be common in Florida and because of this I am especially careful. In one instance a homeowner came to my office and asked me to short sell his property to a specific buyer at the lowest possible price. His wife was the only signer on the promissory note and mortgage and she had assumed all the liability. I shared with him my strategy that by procuring the highest price, we had a better chance of getting lender's approval and of having her released from the deficiency. Even though I explained to him that selling the home for the highest price possible would help his wife, he did not seem to care. His position reeked of fraud to me. I went into my usual probing mode, "Do you already have the buyer? Do you know this person?" To which he responded that he knew the buyer. Then he added, "A lot of people do it." This last statement is what caught my attention. I then bluntly asked, "Do you intend to purchase the property back from him after the short sale?" To which he responded "Yes, everybody does it, so can I." I said, "That is illegal! I'm sorry, but I am not able to help you with this type of transaction."

> Short sale fraud is a crime both at the state and federal levels. It is best, that when in doubt, ALWAYS consult an attorney.

I am so glad I trusted my gut and had the wherewithal to probe and ask these questions. My entire life I have worked hard to remain an elite and ethical professional. If I had allowed someone to trick me into doing a transaction like that I would have felt ashamed. I have no personal desire to risk my license or my liberty, so I politely escorted him out of my office and closed their file.

Some of the telltale signs that short sale fraud might be at play are when the homeowner comes to the listing agent asking to sell the property for the lowest possible price or requests a specific buyer, in spite of the agent bringing in higher offers. If you are an agent reading this book, my advice is to explain to the homeowner that you are trying to help them. If they are obstinate they may have a hidden agenda, so I say terminate the listing. Do not compromise your integrity. Besides, the possible legal troubles are just not worth it.

If you are a realtor listing a short sale property, you are better off if you ask the tough questions up front and immediately. Even if you don't know these conditions exist at the outset, not knowing does not protect you from prosecution. Also, be sure to keep good records of your conversations with everyone to protect yourself and your clients. You never know when you may have to prove you acted properly in the event your transaction is investigated for short sale fraud.

If you are a seller and you believe you have found a creative solution to your mortgage debt problem, make sure to ask the right questions to find out if what you have in mind is legal.

When Tenants Have to Leave

For agents representing the seller or the buyer, make sure there is a clause in the sales contract that tenants must be out before closing. If a tenant still occupies the property at the time of the lender's approval, make sure they are out no later than one day before closing. If this requirement is not satisfied, the buyer is not obligated to close unless the buyer accepts the property with the lease and the tenants. I have had incidents where tenants demanded relocation expenses to move out or have left huge items such as a broken entertainment center. Sellers must make sure the tenants and their possessions are removed prior to the walkthrough.

Removal of Seller's Belongings

Early in my career I worked with some clients who wanted to purchase a distressed property. The property was well kept. A few days prior to closing the sellers requested to leave some big items until after the closing. They verbally agreed to remove the items the day after closing. Since I was new in the business, I negotiated with my clients to agree to the arrangement. A few days after the closing when I went to show the property to the property management company, I found the giant screen TV was left behind because it was broken. Because we had closed the sellers refused to remove the giant TV from the property. Since I represented the buyers and I had negotiated with them to agree to the seller's request, I felt responsible. I was fortunate to have introduced my clients to a property management company willing to work with me. The villa needed some repairs and the property management company agreed to remove the giant TV as a courtesy. Sometimes we just get lucky.

Ex-spouses and Other Stakeholders

In some short sales the seller receives a stipend from the seller's lender. This can be great news, except when there are other stakeholders who might hold the sale hostage. They might demand a share of the proceeds and withhold their signature if they are not compensated. I had one case where the lender had approved $20,000 payable to the seller for relocation expenses. We needed the ex-wife to sign the closing documents. As soon as the ex-wife learned about the $20,000 on the settlement statement, she wanted a share. He eventually gave her a portion so she would sign. But for a short time I felt like I was re-watching *The War of the Roses*—only this time it was live.

When There Are Two Lenders

In a short sale where there are two or more lenders involved, make sure the closing is scheduled before the earliest deadline. If there are any closing delays it may affect one or both of the approved deadlines. If so, the listing agent or the person responsible for negotiating with the lender must get an extension from each of the lenders affected by the new closing date and notify everyone, even if you are still within the deadline of the other lender.

Make sure that all the terms in both approval letters match.

For example, if one approval letter authorizes a commission payment at the maximum rate and the other approval letter reduces the commission, you do not have an agreement and you need to go back and get an agreement from all lenders before closing. Here are some other essential elements that each of the respective lenders' approval letters should contain and the terms must match:

- Payment to the second lender. Both the first lender and the second lender's approval letters should specify the amount paid to the second lender. Make sure the amounts on both letters are the same and they are consistent with the settlement statement.

- Approved buyers. Make sure the spelling of each party's name is the same on the purchase contract, the approval letter, and the settlement statement. Sometimes buyers want to add other individuals to the deed at closing. Any individual you plan to have on the deed needs to be named in the purchase contract and in the approval letters. You can't have one letter from the first lender that approves Carmen Smith as the buyer, and another approval letter from the second lender that approves Carmen Smith and Joseph Jones.

Last Minute Issues at Closing

As you have learned throughout this book, short sales are a bag of surprises that must be dealt with for the transaction to close. And sometimes at the last minute problems show up to derail the short sale. This is where an experienced realtor anticipates issues that can arise and lays out alternate plans to avoid hiccups. The most common ones I've seen are:

- Seller Related
  - The seller stopped paying the condo or homeowners association fees sometime after the short sale process started but didn't communicate that information to

anyone. The closing agent found out when the estoppel letter was requested and association arrears needed to be paid to be able to close the short sale.

- Sellers are not able to vacate the property the day of closing. It must be emphasized to the seller that if they want the short sale to close everything has to be out of the property by the end of the day of closing.

- Buyer Related
  - The funds from the buyer did not arrive until the day of closing in the afternoon. I have been in closings where we've had to get an extension of the closing date or close after business hours to meet the closing deadline.
  - The buyers are not satisfied with the way the house looks at the walkthrough. In situations like this I had to negotiate. There have been times that I have to roll-up my sleeves and clean with the crew just to make the property acceptable to the buyer.
  - The buyers are from out of town and their flight is delayed. If the buyers are from out of town, make sure that you have a backup plan if anything goes wrong. A backup plan could be granting power of attorney to their lawyer, realtor, or someone local who they know and trust to authorize and sign the documents.

The Final Event

The final event occurs once the settlement statement has been signed by all parties, the closing agent has received the funds from the buyer, and the closing agent has wired the funds to the lender and has delivered the original documents executed at closing. Once the lender has received the funds and all documents required on the acceptance letter, the lender then processes the transaction internally. Some lenders issue an email to verify receipt while others do not communicate unless anything is missing. Finally, after the lender clears the funds, the lender sends the satisfaction of mortgage to the closing agent who completes the recording so as to clear the title for the buyer.

Murphy's Law at Work Even After Closing

In short sales sometimes the unthinkable happens. Anything can go wrong, even right after closing. So make sure you keep all closing documents in a secure place where you can find them.

In one instance, the day after closing I received a call from the new owner saying that the front door lock had been changed. Right away I knew the lender's loss mitigation department had forgotten to notify the preservation department that the property had been sold, and the preservation department had gone ahead and changed the locks.

I called the loss mitigation department and was informed that I had to call the preservation department to gain access to the property, which I did. Since we had already closed, I had to bring the new owner as well as the seller to the conference all parties to verify that the property was indeed sold and the new owner was authorized to take possession. After spending over two hours on the phone I was able to resolve the issue.

In another short sale, the week after closing I received a call from a person who claimed to have bought the house at a court auction. It seemed no one at the bank had informed the lender's lawyer to cancel the judicial sale. After the phone conversation I called the closing officer at the bank and explained what had happened. In addition, the lawyer representing my client contacted the foreclosure attorney representing the bank. The issue was rectified. I can only say that was another one of those times when having a lawyer on my side came in handy.

At times short sales remind me of that line from *Forrest Gump* about life being "like a box of chocolates, you never know what you're going to get." Even with the best due diligence and planning, all sorts of issues can arise to delay or derail a transaction.

Therefore, you must keep in mind that receiving an approval letter is an indication for everyone involved to go into "high gear," whether you are the homeowner, buyer, closing agent, or realtor. More importantly, just because the lender has issued an approval letter it does not mean the short sale is successfully closing unless the necessary steps are completely satisfied.

"Success consists of going from failure to failure without loss of enthusiasm."

—Winston Churchill

9

Opening the Door to New Beginnings

This chapter is mainly for the sellers who have gone through a short sale because once the transaction is complete, everyone else involved is back to business as usual. The buyer has purchased a nice property at a great price; the realtors, lenders, HOAs, and closers are on to the next transaction. The seller, however, has a chance to close the door on the old and open a door to a new beginning. The seller may experience mixed emotions for several days after the closing, and some of the old stress triggers may reappear from time to time for several months. It might take a while before the seller remembers that a knock on the door means a friend or family member has come to visit and not the sheriff to serve legal papers.

Forgive Yourself and Move On

A while back I had an elderly client who, throughout the entire process, remained in denial about the fact that the short sale was happening. Even though many people from his church offered to help him make the transition, he took no steps to find another place to live. Before we could get to closing, he committed suicide.

Although an end this tragic is rare, it doesn't have to happen to anyone. The key is to keep an objective perspective. No matter how much you love your home, it is not who you are, and the sooner you can separate the property from your identity the easier it will be to leave it and move on.

The happiest people are the ones who learn to let it go. The house they sold as the short sale transaction is now left behind and they move on. Mindset is everything—if the person believes they can rebound, they do, and they come back stronger than ever. Once a short sale is complete, individuals have a chance to start looking at how to rebuild their lives. I had one client who, within two years of the short sale, was able to buy a new home even higher-end than the one they had to short sell.

Whatever you do don't become a masochist and beat yourself up. Learn from the mistake and make it work for you. Every successful person has had investments that didn't go as well as they wanted. They did not quit and they kept moving forward.

This is the time to move on to a new chapter in your life. Life's ups and downs come in cycles. Even if you have to modify the way you live for a while, it is not the end of the world. Another door will open with an opportunity right in front of you. I know because I have been there.

Embrace the Opportunity

I often see clients make significant changes after just a few months. Some of my clients choose to uproot and move out of state, perhaps closer to grandchildren or to pursue a new business opportunity, and some even move abroad. Some people discover that they prefer a smaller, simpler house with less upkeep. Others decide to rent and take two or three years to reevaluate their lives while they build their wealth again.

I had one client who was trying to develop a new venture which she couldn't pursue as long as she kept her house. Her mortgage took so much of her income and she didn't have enough funds to leave her job and pursue her dreams. When she was downsized from her job, she had no choice but to sell the home. The short sale freed her to pursue her new venture with passion.

Another set of clients had lived alongside celebrities in one of the most exclusive communities in the country, and after their short sale, decided to downsize and change the focus of their lives to charitable work.

Purchasing Again

There are some lenders that have "Second Chance" loans and allow the purchase of a home after eighteen months. I have had clients who have been able to purchase another home just one year after closing a short sale. I am not a mortgage broker, but I have seen that it depends on how fast an individual can turn their financial situation around and save enough money to put twenty to twenty-five percent into a down payment.

> I love the quote "Every day is a journey, and the journey itself is home" from Matsuo Basho because it gives you an insightful view.

Relief—The Burden Is Lifted and Fear Is Gone

Some time ago one of my clients was having a very difficult time letting go of his beloved home and at times I could feel his pain. It seemed he felt like he was divorcing those years filled with memories attached to his beloved home. This man is a great communicator and even though his words did not express the sadness he was carrying, his persona was unable to disguise his discontentment. The day of the closing, my client seemed overwhelmed with sadness even though the sky was so blue and there were barely any clouds. I remember telling him that someday he would be so glad he made this decision. But his eyes only showed disbelief in my words.

I can only say the universe has a funny way of communicating. The day after the closing, the new owners were in the garage and heard a loud noise. The old water heater had finally given up. If this had happened the day before, it would have been my client's problem and they could ill afford the expense. But for the new homeowners, it was going to be replaced anyway. As for my client, he was relieved that it happened after closing. This incident, while not monumental, confirmed that he had made the right decision. When I spoke to him shortly after, all he talked about was his new grandchild. That house had become merely a part of his past.

People do move on!

The Future Relationship

Realtors tend to move from one transaction to another, but for short sale clients, their memories of you are positive and lasting because you helped them through one of the toughest times in their lives. If I help them find a new rental I sometimes show up with a small gift and stay in touch. I send them updates on anything related to life after a short sale.

On occasion, after completing a short sale, I have selected a host of photos of the home and sent it off to be compiled in a bound book dedicated to the seller. Two clients who had to short sell their home not only raised their children there, but the home also had some historical significance. As they were browsing through the book tears rolled down their cheeks. They were so appreciative to receive the book that preserved their memories. I'm told the book became a permanent fixture on the coffee table in their new home.

Getting to know my clients afforded me the opportunity to learn of the many memories they had of their home. Watching them move out on the day of closing reminded me of watching my child ride a bike for the first time. I could see both exhilaration and trepidation in their eyes. I knew the memories were strong and hard to let go.

"Always do right. This will gratify some people and astonish the rest."

—Mark Twain

10

Home Marketing Strategies

If you are planning to sell your home, reading this chapter may help you gain an understanding of all that goes on behind the scenes to attract the most opportune buyer. The common perception that working with a realtor is as simple as listing a home and putting the listing on the MLS is far from reality, especially if you are serious about selling your home. A qualified buyer will be willing and able to make an offer and go above and beyond the norm to get to closing because they identify themselves with your home or believe it has potential.

What Sellers Need to Know

As I have indicated throughout this book, "A successful sale is the product of the realtor's time, dedication, and experience expended BEFORE the house is listed." For a homeowner choosing the right realtor can be the difference between selling your home for the highest and best price with terms that weigh heavily in your favor, or costing you tens of thousands of dollars in equity because it took months or years to get a buyer. The right agent is a marketing consultant who is willing to spend money on extensive target marketing of your home instead of simply marketing themselves and their past achievements. Many years ago merely placing the listing on the MLS and putting a photo of the listing on the glass that could be seen from the sidewalk facing the street was enough to sell a property. But it has not been that way for years. A mix of offline and online target marketing is the way to go today.

Even before we post on the MLS we explore a great diversity of tools and systems to grab the attention of those interested in purchasing the property you are intending to sale. In today's global market it is important to consider traditional and new media as part of the property marketing plans: photography, social networks, MLS, real estate websites, magazine ads, electronic and physical brochures, direct target mailings, the brokerage community, international marketing, flyers, and more. What tools and/or systems should you and your realtor use? In my opinion, you need to use as many as possible.

Visual Aids: Photography

When you hear the expression, a picture is worth a thousand words, have you ever wondered what it actually means? In fact, while discussing the importance of visual aids with Mike Parkinson, author of Billion Dollar Graphics, he explained that "visual aids are processed 100 times faster than text, graphics quickly affect our emotions, and our emotions greatly affect our decision-making." Photography can act as a narrative, giving you a story into the house and help you imagine yourself within that narrative. Bad photography can also create a narrative, though one where you imagine yourself NOT within it.

In my opinion every listing should have professional photos taken; the idea of taking photos with a smart phone does not sit well with me. The MLS is filled with bad photos and it speaks volumes about the lack of professionalism of those agents. Bad photos lead to low offers and it will take longer to sell the property. Go to your MLS or realtor.com to see them. For extraordinary examples of photos gone awry, go to the following sites:

- http://terriblerealestateagentphotos.com
- http://badmlsphotos.com
- http://www.telegraph.co.uk/news/picturegalleries/
  howaboutthat/11444039/Could-you-live-here-21-
  terrible-estate-agent-photographs.html?frame=3216517

Good photography, on the other hand, encourages buyers to call because it triggers emotions and conveys the beauty of the residence in a way that resonates with the potential buyer. Photos that portray the lifestyle of the residence must be an integral part of the marketing strategy and not an afterthought.

I have made it a practice to attend my listings' photo shoots because it allows me to work closely with each photographer. Since interior design is one of my hobbies I collect *Veranda*, *Architectural Digest*, and *LUX*, as well as other interior design magazines. I recall that when I started in this business I found a lot of ideas and inspiration by browsing through their photos. At times I brought a magazine to show the lifestyle that I intended to convey. And still today if I have ideas or suggested angles for the photographer to use, I make sure to share them with the photographer. In the end, it helps achieve the vision I have of the home and the lifestyle that will resonate with the right buyer. A great example is when I ask the photographer to take a photo of the patio table. Imagine the patio with wine strategically placed as you overlook the Intracoastal with a boat docked behind you. This image exudes the South Florida lifestyle and is inviting to any buyer.

I know an agent who had to learn the importance of photography the hard way. This agent shared with me that when she started in the real estate business, she sent one of her clients a listing without photos because the listing had a beautiful description. For her, the description of the property made it seem perfect. It had the desired square feet of living space and it was in the neighborhood her client wanted. Upon receipt of the listing her client called back infuriated. To her surprise her client had seen the house with his previous agent. In spite of the beautiful description the property was a handyman special and the buyer was not looking for that type of challenge. This agent learned that listings without a photo or with poor quality photos are a proverbial red flag and should be further investigated prior to sending the listing to any potential buyer.

Photos are an integral part of your real estate marketing strategy, therefore, it is crucial to keep the following in mind:

1. Good photography helps create the story that attracts potential buyers.

2. Bad photos repel buyers from seeing the property.

3. Deceitful photos are a waste of everyone's time.

Visual Aids: Electronic and Printed Brochures

Brochures are an opportunity to describe and demonstrate the lifestyle the property represents. This concept is not new and is a standard marketing tool in the luxury and ultra-luxury real estate markets, and any property that is being sold can benefit from this practice. I take the time to describe what is unique and special about the property because a brochure is a great tool to attract distant buyers who may identify with the home. In a traditional resale a four-page design should suffice.

A word of caution, a property brochure is not intended to market you. To effectively impress prospective buyers, think about what might be important to them. Prospects will have three questions in mind as they evaluate a property:

- What is special about this property?
- What are the features and benefits?
- Does the lifestyle resonate with me?

I personally use a copywriter, but if that is not suitable to you, the best way to start is by identifying that opportune buyer. Then answer the questions or you will lose their attention immediately.

Regardless, a brochure is no different than a presentation and you need to know your audience. Make sure the quality of the brochure reflects the quality of the property. But do not forget to communicate the negatives of the property. Laurie Moore-Moore, founder of the Institute for Luxury Home Marketing, calls it "the principle of sacrifice." This is not about getting massive numbers of buyers into the property. An effective marketing approach strives to match the property with the most opportune buyer.

In the luxury market my brochures tell a complete story and some have over sixteen pages with beautiful professional photos. I am a proponent of an electronic version of the brochure for those who want everything to be at the touch of a button. By now my clients expect it, so I do not want to disappoint them.

Visual Aids: Video/Virtual Tours

Consumers, whether they are high-net-worth individuals or market consumers, love videos. You just need to look at the popularity of YouTube. When virtual tours debuted they had a competitive edge. Much has changed since then, and today it has become the standard in real estate marketing services. Whether it is a series of photos put together in a video highlighting the home's rooms and features or the 360-degree panoramic views that allow the viewer to get a feel of the property, marketing videos are a must.

Just remember that videos or virtual tours follow the same rationale as photos. This is not a do-it-yourself project unless you have purchased the right tools, like Animoto or Magisto. Both video applications work on iPhones. It is my belief that the only way to go is to hire a professional to create the video. It is always important to identify the audience, determine the needed tools, and spend the money to get the results you want.

Visual Aids: Property-Specific Website

Depending on their personalities, buyers will value data and statistics or stories. Therefore, a property-specific website provides the flexibility to engage the potential buyer in a way that is well received by them, no matter the personality type. You can have the potential buyer access all the marketing tools from the property website, including social networks. Tools like www.agencylogic. com and www.listingsunlimited.com are some of the various applications to choose from when creating a property website. There are several caveats and everything I said about the other visual aids applies here. Remember that through marketing you are selling a lifestyle. Hire a professional to produce quality websites if that is not your expertise.

> Even if you are not in the luxury market these concepts could be applied with success in any price point.

In the end every house has a story. The MLS and various real estate websites provide limited information for any listing. A property-specific website allows you to create a repository where buyers can view all the information needed to make a decision. Particulars on a property website may include neighborhood information, restrictions, information about membership equity (if the community is one of those), deeds, property plans, etc. In addition, properly packaged and positioned properties may cause the seller to increase their "perceived" value of services rendered by you as their agent. And this is extremely important when working in the luxury market.

Visual Aids: Mini-Movies

The use of mini-movies or "lifestyle presentation films" to market luxury real estate is a fairly new concept. This marketing tool invokes emotions in the right buyer, providing a psychological connection with the home. The focus of these films is on the benefits of a lifestyle and not necessarily on the home's amenities. Mini-movies allow the true essence of the home to come through.

The process is complex because it requires a production value complete with story lines, actors, musical scores, and even aerial cinematography. Typically, these mini-movies are used to win a listing or an extension of one. For example, if a home has been on the market a while and the sellers are considering a price reduction, the cost of a mini-movie is just a fraction of the cost of reducing the list price. In addition, this type of marketing could attract the most opportune buyer to the property in a fraction of the time. These mini-movies will engage the right buyer immediately because even though the property is the main character, the plot creates an atmosphere the buyer can identify with. One of my favorite mini-movies was created for the sale of a residence in Colorado: 529 Benchmark Drive Mountain Village. The mini-movie can be viewed on YouTube: https://youtu.be/UjNXt-GF3dXs. The residence is stunning. The movie shows a snowy paradise with the grandfather putting everyone's phones in a large wooden box, steering everyone's focus to the ambience which includes hot tubs, crackling fireplaces, skiing, and other activities associated with snow. It is brilliant! It almost made me want to ditch my home in Boca Raton for the pure white snow of the mountains, until I remembered why I left Massachusetts twenty-five years ago and never looked back. After all, I'm an islander from the Caribbean and I like the tropics. But for a brief moment that powerful video drew me into the mountain lifestyle.

Brokerage Community

Since there is always a chance the buyer may come through another realtor, I always make sure to use e-blasts to announce new listings and to provide updates to other agents in the area, both nationally and internationally. I also hold open houses for brokers because these are a great way to create momentum while energizing the brokerage community. The objective is to capture the attention of other agents in such a way that when they go to their respective offices they tell their colleagues about the great property they just viewed.

Broker open houses are a great opportunity to obtain professional feedback on how well your home shows and to ensure that the real-life experience of the property matches the marketing strategy. It is also a means to get objections from agents, which can be shared with the seller. Another objective of broker open houses is to start managing the psychology of the sale by giving those agents sound bites or rebuttals to take away in an effort to overcome possible objections. Anticipating objections and setting the right expectations is one of my responsibilities. In the end, as the listing agent I am responsible for providing the other agents with information that will facilitate the sale of the property in the least amount of time and at the highest price possible.

I have had sellers who do not allow broker open houses because they do not see the value. In those circumstances I have to explain the value. It is my opinion that a broker open house allows agents who see the property to identify a possible fit to the needs of one of their clients. Broker open houses also cut down traffic into the property and contribute to the momentum when the property enters the market. You may be asking yourself why do they cut traffic? It is simple, if I am working with a client and I know they are looking for a 4 bedroom home and even though the house I previewed in the open house has on the MLS 4 bedroom but one of the bedrooms was converted, I will share with my client and most of the time my client do not want to see a house that do not meet the criteria. That translates to less traffic. If you are listing a luxury home, it is always a good idea to hold invitation-only open houses for a select number of power agents.

Public Open Houses

Even though I have held public open houses, this is my least favorite marketing tool. Some people who attend open houses are looking for interior design ideas or are curiosity seekers rather than serious buyers. In one of my listings I had an incident where a group came in together and one of the members of the group started to wander off alone. I always have at least one other agent with me so I was able to catch up with the individual who was in the middle of opening the medicine cabinet in the master bath. I have no idea what the reason was but I did not like it and asked the person to stay with the rest of the group. On the other hand, I have held open houses where even though the viewers were not interested in buying, they had friends or family who were the perfect fit. I listed one property that showed so well viewers were telling others in the neighborhood all about it. The house went under contract the following week.

There is no right or wrong, but I find that in very exclusive homes it is best not to hold public open houses and show by appointment only.

Real Estate Websites and Social Networks

Even though social networking remains a growing phenomenon, I still hear some agents tell me their clients are not on the Internet. Both high-net-worth individuals and mass-market consumers surf the Internet, regardless of their background. Furthermore, ninety-two percent of buyers used the Internet in some way in their home search process, according to the National Association of Realtors.[5] Today's consumers start their home search by looking online for properties, pre-qualifying them by looking at the photos, virtual tours, property movies, and real estate websites prior to calling an agent. Given the need for maximum exposure a property must be in as many sites as possible.

Social networks are great tools to connect with potential buyers, as well as sellers, and to create company and service awareness. Furthermore, I find social networks an effective way to prospect the affluent and a way to communicate and keep relationships. I personally use Facebook for my company for several reasons. First, I advertise our services and write blogs that interest my customers related to the real estate industry. Second, I like to send words of affirmation to my friends, fans, colleagues, and clients because I believe in promoting positive thoughts. It is just my personal

---

[5]   "Home Buyer and Seller Generational Trends Report 2015," *National Association of* Realtors, March 2015, Exhibits 3-7, http://www.realtor.org/sites/default/files/reports/2015/2015-home-buyer-and-seller-generational-trends-2015-03-11.pdf.

belief. Finally, I like to post photos of wonderful architectural design concepts on Pinterest. My company places listings for consumers to view on social networks and on over one hundred local, national, and international websites. Why social networks? Because almost half of US consumers now spend forty-seven minutes of their day on social networks, according to the Nielsen Consumer Report.[6]

I view the use of social networks the same way as social events where the purpose is to connect with other people. I do not take business cards with me, and instead I collect business cards or contact information from others. I do not see dollar signs on every face, and moreover, I see a potential ally who may work with me in the future, provided they have a disposition that matches mine. There is nothing I dislike more than when a person at one of these events comes up to you, says hello, hands you their business card, and walks away as if their elevator pitch just won them a new client. I was raised in a relationship-based culture where you take the time to get to know the other person. And only after you identify that your work ethics align do you seek to create a lasting, profitable work relationship. I am well aware that is not the way most people conduct business in the US. But unlike other industries, real estate is all about emotions and emotion is why people buy real estate.

Direct Target Mailing

Just like any other marketing tool in real estate, direct mail campaigns have the ability to capture the recipient's attention even when they are not actively looking in the market. But you

Only 8% of recent home sales were FSBO sales. This is the lowest share recorded since 1981, according to the NAR Profile of Buyers and Sellers 2015 report

---

[6] "The U.S. Digital Consumer Report," *Nielsen*, February 10, 2014, http://www.nielsen.com/us/en/insights/reports/2014/the-us-digital-consumer-report.html.

must have the correct copy-written marketing piece with photos that emotionally connects with the type of buyer who will have the highest level of interest and the financial ability to buy. Therefore, you have to make sure you match the mailers to each audience you are seeking to attract. You must understand the people you are targeting to have an idea of what works with them and what doesn't. For example, jargon, designs, and photos that attract boat owners might not attract the demographics you might be targeting for second-home purchases in a golf community away from the coast.

There is also a difference in selling a $700,000 home and a $10 million dollar estate. These are both luxury properties in most locations of the country, but the approach to selling each differs even though both require affluent buyers. The campaign to target the specific type of buyer is directly related to the buyer's financial qualifications, net worth, annual household income, and lifestyle, among other qualifications.

This is how it works. A property with a bundle of amenities commands a value when marketed to the most opportune buyer possible. And, marketing the property to anyone who is in a higher or lower price range than that commanded value would be an absolute waste of your resources and efforts.

International Buyers

Real estate stores wealth safely in the United States; therefore, international homebuyers are eager to invest here. Unlike other parts of the world, real estate in this country provides stability and value appreciation. Wealthy foreign buyers are looking to increase their net worth and secure a better future for themselves and their families. Therefore, they may be willing to pay top dollar for your property. But before you decide to attract them, you need to know a few things.

I have often found that when I get calls from foreign buyers to purchase property, they are not physically here. So they decide to make a purchase based on pictures and videos of the property without physically seeing the property. This is another reason to invest in professional photography.

Foreigners tend to cluster, therefore, you must consider the area where the property is located, its price, and even the health of the economy in the countries where those international buyers are coming from. For example, I used to frequently travel to Venezuela and in those days Venezuelans called Weston, Florida, the area where I lived, "Westonzuela." You can imagine how the name originated. I was not in real estate in those days, but people I knew from Venezuela kept purchasing property in Weston.

The other example I would like to share is that some wealthy Chinese buyers look for investment opportunities in a location where they plan to send their children for higher education. Chinese buyers have the mentality to think years ahead, and they purchase the property way ahead of time while their children are young. If your home is near a university, it would be good to learn the demographics of the students at that university.

In my experience most international buyers pay cash, but some want a mortgage (both investors and those buying vacation homes). If you are a realtor make sure you have established relationships with loan officers of institutions that cater to foreign nationals.

Market your property on international sites like www.world-properties.com and www.real-buzz.com. You could also market the listing on sites specific to the country where you are trying to attract buyers. For example, with some of my listings I have marketed on Juwai.com to attract Chinese buyers.

Go the extra mile by putting yourself in their shoes. For example, it is always helpful to include things like square meters since other countries do not use square footage. Make a complete list of what will stay in the house; do not assume the foreign buyers know. In many countries appliances are not included in the sale of a home.

China has overtaken Canada as the top country of origin for foreign buyers in the U.S., according to NAR 2015 Profile of Home Buying Activity of International Clients.

I won't ever forget the shock I had when purchasing a home in Puerto Rico, so close to the United States and yet so different. In Puerto Rico houses often do not come with appliances, even if it is a luxury home in an exclusive community, and that was a shock to me.

It's All about Connecting

As I have shown throughout this chapter, there are many tools from which to choose. Simply put, it takes a combination of relationships, processes, and the proper tools to get the right buyer. Don't lose focus because in the end it is about the feelings that are evoked within that buyer that determines the sale. I know this may seem simplistic but if you are the seller, take the time to identify that buyer you are envisioning to attract. Then put yourself in their shoes and while at it, envision the feelings you want to evoke when that buyer is walks into a house for the first time. Call it a feeling, a sense of giddiness, or the sound of angels singing. Whatever the feeling the result is the same; finding the perfect home is a special moment, and that is what you want to achieve as you connect with that buyer.

If you, the seller, do not remember I will give you an example and further insight into what goes on in the mind of a buyer. I will share what I remember about my first time buying a house that was not a new construction. The only reason I likely remember is because most of my life I worked with builders but while buying a house in Puerto Rico there was no other choice than to purchase a home that needed some changes to meet my family's lifestyle. The house that drew my attention also had flowery wallpaper in the main areas and it was hideous. The other drawback was, as I previously mentioned, the house came with no kitchen appliances. I was forced to see beyond these limitations.

The same day of the closing the wallpaper was removed in the formal living areas and we shopped for appliances. The rooms looked larger without the wallpaper and like any other buyers, we were happy.

There was another reason that made that neighborhood attractive. After living in the US for so long, the idea of a home with bars on the windows, which is standard in Latin American architecture outside of certain high-end neighborhoods, did not appeal to me. So this neighborhood's lack of barred windows was the first thing that attracted me.

Just think how a home is able to evoke so many memories and establish a connection, and you will begin to understand what I believe a seller should strive to achieve.

How Do You Attract Buyers?

Whether you are an agent or a homeowner looking to find the right buyer for your home you must work closely to identify the uniqueness of the property and benefits to the most opportune buyer. Your home is worth a great deal to the type of buyer who appreciates and needs what it has to offer. Then you need to cross-reference to find those who can afford it. This information is the basis of the target marketing approach used to attract the absolute best quality buyer who would pay the most amount of money with terms acceptable to you, even when those buyers were not actively looking. As I indicated previously: "A successful sale is the product of the realtor's time, dedication, and experience expended BEFORE the house is listed."

This is a situation where the realtors coordinate the process, the sellers move on, and the new homeowners have a home to live in and create new memories. Just remember, this is about everyone winning.

*"Hope and fear cannot occupy the same space.
Invite one to stay."*

—Maya Angelou

11

Where Does the Journey Start?

The strategy depends on what you are trying to achieve. If you are a homeowner, you must first define what you are selling and identify all the great features your home has to offer. It is amenities, location, an outstanding trophy like a historical home, uniqueness like a batting cage or a stable, and other things that are important to that specific buyer you are looking to attract. This list will be used by your agent to ensure a marketing strategy is carefully and artfully drafted to attract the best possible buyers. I recently met a property owner who kept making the same mistake over and over again. This person kept listing the house without selling it. The house was continually overpriced and did not show well for the price point. The house became a revolving door of realtors.

If you are the buyer does your agent understand what is important to you? What are the nice things you want to have but may not be as important? What is your time line? Do you have to sell another property? Are there personal reasons that make it imperative to move within a certain time frame? Are you a haggler and can wait forever? Or are you a serious buyer waiting for the right property?

In the End, This is Just the Beginning

I have demonstrated throughout this book the importance of choosing the right agent. When choosing your realtor be sure that you empathize and can openly work with them. I remember when I went through my short sale and the agent I was using was just there to make a sale. I didn't know any better. Today I know that perhaps I could have worked with an agent who not only knew what I was going through, but one who could empathize and empower me to understand that the day I locked the front door for the last time, a new chapter was opening. This guidance makes a difference because it gives you a different perspective and helps you to be better prepared to move forward.

You have to love working with your agent and the agent has to have the level of expertise needed to guide you. Your agent may be the reason you end up selling your home for as much money as possible and getting terms that weigh heavily in your favor. The wrong agent can cost you tens of thousands of dollars in equity due to price reductions because your home stayed on the market too long. My son, who recently started in this business during the publication of this book, already has the loyalty of some of his clients not only because he is personable, but because he uses his law degree to ensure that he researches every new law that affects real estate and he shares the findings with his clientele. Finally, he treats his customers as if they were family and he goes the extra mile. I didn't have to teach him that business trait because he learned it from watching me with my clients. To me he will always be my wonderful child. I have several customers who seek me out years after a sale to see if we can do business together. I tell you, there is nothing more gratifying than having someone you worked with three years ago call you out of the blue and say, "I am looking to purchase a home, can you help me out?" I use the lessons learned from short sales to ensure that I always put a little more effort into those who are willing to listen and earn the most they can.

And as the owner of the home, it would be advantageous for you to share the selling points and ask the agents you are interviewing how they intend to market your property. Make sure you hire the person who can demonstrate how they will properly expose the uniqueness of your home and maximize it. The right agent is a marketing consultant who spends money on extensive target marketing of your home instead of marketing themselves. It is not about putting the listing on the MLS, as I stated over and over in the previous chapters. There are many tools out there and some are more expensive than others. Target marketing is the way to go today. For example, mini-movies are an effective way, but they cost thousands of dollars because of the choreography and paid actors. This is a great tool for properties in the seven-figure price range.

There are many tools to grab the interest of those interested in purchasing your home, but only agents who invest money, time, and have the knowledge can structure the selling campaign of your home effectively. In business there is a common practice of hiring consultants who provide expertise. Selling your home is no different and therefore, it is crucial to find a realtor who works at that level and acts along the lines of a consultant because they make the process seamless for their clients. This win-win-win or consultative approach allows the agent to not only know how to market a property, but also how to structure the best offer and assist you while negotiating to sell your home with the best terms that are important to you.

This type of agent knows how to give you tips on what works and what does not, instead of telling you how great they are or how many properties they have sold. They are more than just a sales person; they are a true advisor who understands the process thoroughly and puts your needs at the top.

Finally, once you understand what is needed to successfully sell in the current market, you can move to the next step. Are you ready now or do you have to take some steps in preparation to sell at a later time? These are the choices that you must make and that is why it is important that you find an agent who can help you look at all the variables. The movie character Gordon Gekko is famously quoted as saying that "greed is good," and in this country we accept a certain level of capitalism with pride, but we cannot forget what binds us together more deeply than money.

I love watching *Shark Tank*. If you have never seen the show, you should watch it at least once. Often times the investors are looking at the bottom line, but more often than you can imagine, the investors look at the people soliciting them with a certain kindness and empathy because they are looking for that X factor that can't be explained. I remember watching an episode where a veteran was making a pitch that seemed like a reasonable business venture. Two of the "sharks" listened to the proposition and while stating that the venture was a little too low end for their tastes, they thought the idea had merit. However, they were so taken aback by the person's veteran status and positive attitude, they offered to buy a portion of his business to ensure that the person who had served our country would have a regional business that would at minimum make him money while also creating a modest return for the sharks. The businessman sold the investors on his story more than his product. Remember that your story can sell your product effectively. Just like my experience going through a short sale ensures that when I work with distressed homeowners, they know that I come from a position of compassion and understanding.

Why Real Estate

Sometimes we have defining moments in life that move us in ways we never imagined, and 2008 was one of those moments for me. Right after I was downsized I found myself without a role in Corporate America. I had to figure out who I was in this new phase. I must admit this journey has been more than just a career search. I got into real estate at a time when short sales were the law of the land, and I saw short sales as the opportunity to enter an industry that I cared about and I have made it work for me. I grant you, in the beginning, I took every opportunity in real estate that came my way because I didn't know any better. But I was determined to learn and make it in this industry. I knew that if I stayed long enough and used my life's experiences, my determination, creative side, and technical background I would succeed.

One of my favorite quotes from Thomas Edison is, "Opportunity is missed by most people because it is dressed in overalls and looks like work." Even though my opportunity came disguised as a lot of work, I know today, without a doubt, that it was the kind of opportunity that comes once in a lifetime. I found my passion and a job that I love.

I must also remind you to embrace the digital world that we live in. Thanks to this global connection which the Internet facilitates, I met my friend Akansha, a young and spiritual woman who is making a difference in India with young women. She contributed to my journey with her guidance in social media.

If you are a realtor, whether seasoned or new to the industry, recognize the importance of your role in other people's lives. We are fortunate to have the opportunity to help others find a layover (their home) on their journey through life.

Conclusion

For me, a real estate transaction goes beyond closing the sale and it goes beyond the new home or the homeowner. It is all about finding that spiritual connection. It's about the vibes, the feelings, and the emotions that come with it. A home is more than a shelter; it embodies the essence of who you are in body and soul. And that is the reason it is so important to each one of us.

You probably thought *The Art of Real Estate in the Digital Age* was only about real estate, but this book is more than that. *The Art of Real Estate in the Digital Age* is the culmination of everything I've had to overcome and experience to thrive in this industry helping others find their home. Real estate has allowed me to grow as an entrepreneur and to turn lemons into more than lemonade. It has been a symphony of opportunities with friends and family playing their parts to help me grow. Today I understand that high quality marketing coupled with creativity has allowed me to fulfill my own desire for success. We often talk about the American Dream and how anyone can make it, but sometimes we don't realize the opportunities that we are given. This is what *The*

Art of Real Estate in the Digital Age has been all about—learning to recognize when opportunity knocks and how to make the most of it in a way that everyone wins. As you embark on a new journey while considering if you should sell your home or seek new opportunities, I wish you well. *The Art of Real Estate in the Digital Age* helps you embrace change and take the time to look at your opportunities, whether you are a successful businessperson exploring new possibilities or someone who is going through an unexpected hardship. In the end, it is all about finding the light within you that sparks another.

"The only source of knowledge is experience."

—Albert Einstein

Acknowledgements

I decided to write a book quite some time ago, but it never dawned on me the amount of effort it takes. If I have succeeded, it is thanks to the generosity of many people including some of my clients, friends, and my son. Their efforts and support were instrumental to the completion of this book. I am very thankful to each one of them.

At the beginning of the process, writing a book was a lot of fun, but once the novelty wore off, it became a second full-time job. I must say that coming up with 48,735 words is a time consuming proposition!

First, I want to thank my son, Yaveth, for being my best friend. Since his birth he has been my inspiration and support. He was the first person to offer help. His experience writing legal briefs in moot court was invaluable, and his discipline in writing helped organize my thoughts before writing not only the first draft, but also when I needed someone to give me feedback on my ideas. He was the one who always asked, "Where is the funny stuff?"

Next, I have to thank my parents, especially my mom for naming me Norka. Knowing the etymology of my name has driven me to reach higher with each passing day.

I want to thank my dear Howard for believing in me. Over the past two years, he has given me the time to write without complaint. When the initial manuscript was near completion, he reviewed it for the first time. Thanks to his inquisitive mind, I added more content by explaining things that were obvious to me but unknown to readers. He also acted as my legal consultant.

I also thank my friend, Joanna Garzilli, for writing the foreword and for putting me in contact with Robin Colucci. I will never forget Robin's kind words after reading my first draft. I asked Robin to be honest with me, and she explained that my draft had a lot of information but it was not engaging. For the following six months, we spoke weekly to shape each chapter.

I am very grateful to my friend Akansha Gautam for introducing me to Kent Gustavson who challenged me to put my heart into this project.

Last, my thanks to all that contributed during the final stretch. Lucia Brown, the crack proofreader who did an amazing job. Debbie O'Byrne, who once she understood my artistic and demanding nature, superseded all my expectations while designing the cover of this book. Finally, my Publicist and Book Marketing Specialist, Denise Cassino. I am very grateful for all her efforts, guidance and for putting me in contact with people to get over the final hurdle to publish this book.

Glossary of Terms Frequently Used in Real Estate Sales

Abstract Title: condensed history of various activities affecting ownership of a parcel of land, starting with the original grant and including all subsequent conveyances and encumbrances affecting the real estate property. See **Title Search**.

Arms-Length Transaction Affidavit: ensures that all parties involved in the sale transaction are acting in their own self-interest independently and have no family or business relationship to any other party. Violation of this affidavit carries federal criminal penalties.

A-quality: property with degree of excellence with distinctive attributes or characteristics.

Broker Price Opinion (BPO): estimated value of a property as determined by a licensed real estate agent. Usually, in short sales, this agent is hired by the lender.

Clear Title or Marketable Title: in any property sale, this refers to the uncontested and unencumbered ownership of real property.

Closing Disclosure: replaced the HUD-1 Settlement Statement and the Truth-in-Lending Act (TILA) disclosure in October 2015.

Comparative Market Analysis (CMA): evaluation based on researching relevant properties that are near a property intended for sale or purchase. It establishes a price estimate based on current market activity that can be used as a pricing guide.

Debt Service: the cash that is required for a particular time period to cover the repayment of interest and principal on a debt. In addition to interest and principal, it may also include arrearages, late fees, and other costs.

Deed: the document that is used to transfer title (ownership) or an interest in real property to another person. The deed must include the legal description of the real property, name the party transferring the property (*grantor*), and the party receiving the property (*grantee*). It has to be signed, witnessed, and notarized by the grantor. To complete the transfer (conveyance), the deed must be recorded in the office of the County Recorder or Recorder of Deeds.

Deed in Lieu: also called "cash for keys." The lender forgives the balance of the debt in exchange of the borrower vacating the property and turning over the deed. It's a voluntary conveyance of title back to the lender. In order to qualify, the property must have no other liens or obligations other than the one to the primary note holder.

Default: occurs when the borrower does not meet the loan terms.

Deficiency: when the sale or disposition of the property fails to generate sufficient revenue to pay the debt service in full.

Deficiency Judgment: refers to a lender's judgment against the borrower for the deficiency. This judgment is recorded in the public record against the borrower.

Distressed Property: properties that are at risk of foreclosure due to non-payment of the mortgage and/or other liens placed against the property.

Escrow: in a real estate sale transaction the primary purpose of escrow is to hold something of value, usually money, until certain conditions are met. The objective is for the real estate title transfer or closing settlement. Depending on the state, the escrow may be held by a lawyer, real estate company, or title company often overseeing a real estate transaction, from initial deposit to final funding, to ensure a smooth process.

Estoppel Letter: document that outlines information regarding a property owner's current financial standing with the community association, including payment amounts, amounts due, and assessments in progress or projected.

Fair Market Value (FMV): estimated price that real estate property would sell for on the open market.

Flopping: an illegal and unethical scheme in which a real estate agent representing a buyer gives the seller's lender an artificially low value of the property, and then sells it for that lower price to their buyer, ignoring legitimate higher offers. The real estate agent and the buyer then sell the home for the higher market value and share the profits.

Forbearance: a form of short-term repayment relief granted by the lender or creditor in lieu of forcing a property into foreclosure.

Foreclosure: a legal process in which a lender exercises its right to force the sale of a property and attempt to recover its losses when the borrower fails to meet the terms of the loan. Ten days after the foreclosure sale, the clerk of court issues a Certificate of Title and the new owner can take immediate possession.

Foreclosure Judgment: a court order in favor of the holder of the promissory note and mortgage. Contained within the court order are the required sums the borrower must pay by a certain date or the property will be sold in accordance with that court's foreclosure process, known as a judicial sale.

Foreclosure Judicial Sale: also referred to as a foreclosure sale or judicial sale date. After the lender obtains a foreclosure judgment from the courts, within that judgment the court will order a specific date and time for the sale of the property. These sales are currently conducted on the Internet through a bidding process.

Forgiveness of Debt: the Mortgage Debt Relief Act of 2007 generally allows taxpayers to exclude income from the discharge of debt on their principal residence. Debt reduced through mortgage restructuring, as well as mortgage debt forgiven in connection with a foreclosure, qualifies for the relief. This provision applies to debt forgiven in calendar years 2007 through 2014. Up to $2 million of forgiven debt is eligible for this exclusion ($1 million per person if married and filing separately). The exclusion does not apply if the discharge is due to services performed for the lender or any other reason not directly related to a decline in the home's value or the taxpayer's financial condition.

Great Recession: applies to both the US recessions which officially lasted from December 2007 to June 2009, and the ensuing global recession of 2009. The economic slump began when the US housing market went from boom to bust and large amounts of mortgage-backed securities and derivatives lost significant value.

Hardship Criteria: to qualify for a short sale, the borrower must be able to demonstrate hardship. Qualifying hardships may come from a number of causes, such as personal and economic decline, long-term illness, high medical expenses, divorce, and/or the death of a primary breadwinner. All of these may satisfy the criteria of "hardship" and allow the lender to approve a short sale.

Homestead Exemption: in Florida, the homestead exemption law precludes any lender, such as credit card companies, auto loan financing companies, gambling institutions, and others, from seizing or forcing the sale of a property that is the homesteader's primary residence. Thus, lenders require that the homesteader waive or release the exemption with the signing of a mortgage.

HUD-1: commonly referred to as the Settlement or Closing Statement. Regulated and enforced by the Department of Housing and Urban Development (HUD), it is the standard form used in all federally regulated real estate transactions in the United States. The HUD-1 itemizes all the costs of the transaction for both the buyer and seller. In a short sale, the seller's mortgage servicing company must always approve the fees on the seller side, which are paid out of the sale proceeds.

Lien: a legal claim on a property by a lender or other entity (called the *lien holder*) against a property owner who owes money.

Loan Modification: a permanent change in the terms between a borrower and lender, which allows the loan to be reinstated and most often results in a payment the borrower can afford.

Loss Mitigation Department: is a division or department of a financial institution charged with the task of minimizing the losses incurred in the event of defaulted upon loans and foreclosures.

Mortgage Debt Relief Act: see **Forgiveness of Debt.**

Negative Equity: when the market value of a property falls below the debt service that is due pursuant to the terms of the note and mortgage securing the property.

Net Proceeds: the amount of cash remaining from a property sale, minus settlement charges associated with the transfer and payment of the lender's debt service. In a short sale, the settlement charges, including real estate commissions, must be approved by the seller's lender.

Payoff: total amount required to satisfy the terms of a mortgage loan and pay off a mortgage debt. Payoff amount is different from the current balance, which is the amount owed as of the date on a monthly statement. Payoff amount includes the payment of any interest owed through the day the borrower pays off the loan.

Preservation Department: a department within a lending institution charged with the task of preventing damage to properties that are in foreclosure. In addition, they are responsible for securing a property to prevent or discourage re-entry by its former occupants or trespassers, both of whom can damage the property and may require legal proceedings for their removal. The department usually hires a local property preservation company to secure a property (changing locks, boarding up), remove debris, and/or provide property maintenance (winterizing, cutting grass, repairing roof leaks), and rehabilitation if needed.

Promissory Note: a legal instrument (more particularly, a financial instrument), in which one party (the *maker* or *issuer*) promises in writing to pay a sum of money to the other (the *payee*), either at a fixed or determinable future time or on demand of the payee, under specific terms.

Settlement/Closing: the final event in a real estate sale, which usually takes place in the office of an attorney or a title insurance closing agent. In a short sale, once the seller's lender issues an approval letter and the buyer obtains financing or produces the funds in cash, all of the parties agree upon a time to sign the documents.

Servicer: a financial institution that manages loans for investors, including billing, payments, accounting, communications with borrowers, and other tasks. Some investors/lenders act as their own servicers while others hire outside companies to manage their loan portfolios.

Service Transfer: the owner of the note transfers the servicing of a loan from one servicer to another servicer.

Short Sale: the sale of a real estate property negotiated with the approval of the seller's lender that agrees to accept a payoff that is less than the debt service.

Short Sale Approval Letter: the lender's agreement to accept a short sale payoff. The letter defines exactly what the lender expects from the seller. It lays out the following terms: acceptable sale price, maximum allowable commissions, maximum closing costs, minimum net proceeds, and closing date, among other considerations. Not every short sale approval letter contains a release of liability. In fact, some approval letters don't address release of liability at all.

Third Party Authorization (TPA): in a short sale transaction, all parties involved must sign a TPA for the seller's lender, allowing its employees to disclose the seller's personal information to real estate agents, attorneys, and anyone else who needs to be privy to such data. This form releases the lender from violating any federal privacy laws.

Title Search: a title search is conducted to review the chain of title ownership and to detail who must sign off so the seller can convey a clear and marketable title to the buyer. Failure of the seller to convey a marketable title will result in the closing agent returning the buyer's lender's funds and terminating the transaction.

Quitclaim Deed: a document that transfers the interest in a real property in which the grantor is vested by removing their name from the title. This does not relieve the signer of their portion of the debt if they are also a signer on the loan.

Underwater Mortgage: a mortgage with a higher balance than the current value of the home. This situation prevents the homeowner from selling the home unless they provide personal funds to pay the difference to satisfy the lender's debt service, or get approved to seek a short sale. This deficiency also lowers the homeowner's ability to refinance in most cases.

Bibliography

Consumer Financing Protection Bureau.
http://www.consumerfinance.gov.

The Free Dictionary by Farlex.
http://www.freedictionarydefinitions.com.

Garner, Bryan A. *Black's Law Dictionary, Ninth Edition*, Eagan: Thomson West, 2009.

The Internal Revenue Service. https://www.irs.gov.

Investopedia. http://www.investopedia.com.

Travel China Guide. https://www.travelchinaguide.com.

Wikipedia. https://www.wikipedia.org.

Other Sources

"2015 AFIRE Annual Foreign Investment Survey," *Association of Foreign Investors in Real Estate*, http://afire.membershipsoftware. org/files/Final%20Main%20Press%20Release(1).docx.

Carlyle, Erin. "Most Expensive U.S. Home Sale Ever: Connecticut Estate Goes for $120 Million," *Forbes*, April 16, 2014, http://www. forbes.com/sites/erincarlyle/2014/04/16/copper-beech-farm-for-120-million-is-americas-new-most-expensive-home-sale/.

"Home Buyer and Seller Generational Trends Report 2015," *National Association of Realtors*, http://www.realtor.org/sites/ default/files/reports/2015/2015-home-buyer-and-seller-genera-tional-trends-2015-03-11.pdf.

The Institute for Luxury Home Marketing is the premier independent authority in training and designation for real estate agents working in the luxury residential market. The Institute awards the Certified Luxury Home Marketing Specialist designation for luxury home marketing to agents who demonstrate exceptional sales performance standards, http://www.luxuryhomemarketing.com/real-estate-agents/home.html.

Christopher Kai, networking expert and author of *Big Game Hunting: Networking with Billionaires, Executives and Celebrities*, http://christopherkai.com/.

Mike Parkinson, author of the *Billion Dollar Graphics* books, http://www.BillionDollarGraphics.com.

Barb Schwarz is the creator of Home Staging® and the Accredited Staging Professional Master (ASPM) Designation for Realtors®, http://www.stagedhomes.com/.

"The U.S. Digital Consumer Report," *Nielsen*, February 10, 2014, http://www.nielsen.com/us/en/insights/reports/2014/the-us-digital-consumer-report.html.

Figure 1. Davies, David. *Adjusting Floor Numbers to Avoid Bad Luck in a Chengdu Hotel* (Photograph). 2004. Source: Museum Fatigue Online, https://museumfatigue.org (Jun 13, 2016).

Figure 2. *Leading extra-realistic virtual staging and interior visualization company in NYC* (Photograph). Source: Leonard Minsky, CEO of Hasten, Inc. Online, https://www.hasten.me (Jun 27, 2016).

Cover Photo. Feld, Howard A. MLS Real Estate Photography. 2015.

About the Author

Norka Parodi is a real estate broker in Boca Raton, FL. She was formerly a Fortune 500 executive with a track record for reviving underperforming organizations. She holds a bachelor degree in Computer Science from the Inter American University of Puerto Rico and graduated Magna Cum Laude. Norka specializes in Luxury Home Sales and was awarded the prestigious 2015 *Best Marketing Campaign for a Property* by Leaders in Luxury. Norka is also a Million Dollar Guild member and now serves in the 2016 Leaders in Luxury Advisory Board.

After years of success, Norka is taking her inspirational message, via public speaking engagements, to corporations and special interest groups. As a business woman, she has the power blue-print for initiating and completing business transactions on a global level. Norka is a MUST have speaker for businesses who want to penetrate the international market and experience exponential global growth.

www.ingramcontent.com/pod-product-compliance
Lightning Source LLC
Chambersburg PA
CBHW050528190326
41458CB00045B/6751/J

* 9 7 8 0 9 9 7 7 7 5 0 2 0 *